The Home Inspection Guide for Do-It-Yourself Home Buyers

John Wade and Keith Banger

ISBN: **978-1508902942**
ISBN 13: **1508902941**

Introduction

I began writing this book several years ago. It started as an informational guide for newly hired home inspectors, because I found it difficult to hire and train new inspectors in a comprehensive manner about the many different things to look for while doing a home inspection. After using this book and training some very successful inspectors (who are still working for me today!), we decided the vast amount of data we had, from the thousands of inspections we've performed over more than the past fifteen years, might be a valuable resource for the public and other home inspection companies.

When people begin the process of buying a new home, out-of-pocket expenses can add up. In an attempt to save some money up-front, many buyers decide to do their own inspections and tend to miss several major problems that can be costly and even dangerous after they buy the home.

The book you hold in your hands is the culmination of many years of experience in the industry, condensed into a form we hope is easy for the average person to use—high-quality pictures and easy-to-understand descriptions of problems in real-life scenarios. It was written for the many do-it-yourselfers out there trying to save hundreds of dollars by inspecting their own homes, those who want to be a knowledgeable "second set of eyes" during a home inspection performed by a professional inspector, those who want to pre-inspect a home they intend to buy or sell, and even people who are thinking about going into the home inspection business on their own. Even though we show over 700 photos in this book and describe a multitude of problems you can find while doing a home inspection, as professionals we still run into new and different problems and scenarios weekly. Remember that even though we made every attempt to be as comprehensive as possible, no guide covers every possible problem, and I will always recommend hiring a professional.

As a professional home inspector with fifteen years of experience, I always encourage my customers to be with me through the entire inspection process. If you are a home buyer and have studied this book, your inspector should appreciate the extra set of eyes, because a home inspector's ultimate goal is to do the very best he or she can do for the buyer.

If you are a home buyer who insists on doing your own inspection, or you are interested in becoming a professional home inspector, you need to take the time to study this book carefully and bring it with you so you can apply the knowledge directly during your inspection. Check out the chapter titled "How to Use This Book—and What You Should Do After the Home Inspection" on page 8 to learn how to best utilize the vast amount of knowledge in this book.

My goal for this book is to provide you with the most comprehensive and easy-to-use information about home inspections, so that you and your family can be successful, happy, and safe in your home purchase. This is what I care most about as a home inspector and as an author.

I wish you the best of luck in your home-buying experience. If you have any questions, concerns, feedback, or success stories, please feel free to connect with us on our website, www.DoItYourselfHomeInspections.com.

To Your Home-Inspection Success...
John Wade—Professional Home Inspector

Contents

Chapter 1
Why Should You Hire a Professional Home Inspector and What Questions Should You Ask When Doing So?

We recommend that everybody buying a home, whether the home is old or new, hire a professional home inspector. Even if you read through this book very carefully, study every photo we have presented, and apply the information to a thorough inspection of the home, you still do not have the years of experience necessary to find all the problems in the two to three hours that you will be at the home doing the inspection.

Yes, you will become much more knowledgeable than the average home buyer, which will help you incredibly, but why not take that knowledge and use it to work with a professional inspector who has inspected hundreds or thousands of homes and has years of experience? Doing so will guarantee your home is better inspected, because it will enable you to be a "second set of eyes" during the inspection. The ultimate goal is for you to find the best home for you and your family.

Here are some questions you should ask any inspector you are thinking about hiring:

1. Are you a licensed, certified inspector? (Remember, not all states demand licensing for home inspectors, so you'll have to find out what your state requires.)

2. Have you taken and passed the National Home Inspectors Exam?

3. Are you insured, and can you prove it? (Many home inspectors are not insured, even when they say they are.)

4. How long have you been in business? (We recommend hiring an inspector with a minimum of three to five years of experience.)

Here are the various types of home inspector certifications:

1. American Society of Home Inspectors (ASHI)

    www.ashi.org

2. National Association of Home Inspectors (NAHI)

    www.nahi.org

3. National Association of Certified Home Inspectors (NACHI)

    www.nachi.org

If an inspector tells you that he or she doesn't need those certifications or doesn't need to have taken and passed the National Home Inspectors exam because he or she is a licensed builder and is trained to repair and build new structures, this is incorrect. Home inspectors are trained to be inspectors and find problems, while builders are trained to build new homes and repair older homes—there is actually a big difference between the two professions. We have some very good friends who have been professional, licensed builders for more than thirty years, and whenever their family members are buying a home they call us to perform the inspection.

Most of the highly qualified inspectors will be priced similarly. You as a buyer can find a low-priced inspector, but remember that you get what you pay for. You are making probably the biggest investment of your life, so hiring the cheapest inspector to save money is not always best (it could cost you more in the long run). Find an inspector who best fits you and the home you are looking to purchase and who has the highest possible qualifications.

Chapter 2
How to Use This Book—and What You Should Do After the Home Inspection

Whether you do the home inspection yourself or hire a professional, you should know what to do with your newfound knowledge both during and after the inspection. How do you apply the home-inspection findings to a real-world scenario? That's what this chapter is all about.

First, start by heading over to our website at **www.DoItYourselfHomeInspections.com** and getting a free copy of our "DIY Home Inspection Checklist." This will help you as you complete your home inspection.

Scenario #1: You're a home buyer with a freshly signed purchase agreement. You're working with a professional real estate agent, and you hire a professional home inspector.

When you hire a professional home inspector, let him or her know that you plan on being present for and participating in the entire home inspection with the inspector. Use the information in this book, and stay in the same area as the inspector so you can discover issues together rather than interfering with the inspection process. We have laid out the information in the book in an order that works best for us and that we think will work best for you, but other inspectors may prefer a different sequence. This is completely fine as long as the entire home is inspected during the process.

Remember, no matter how experienced your home inspector is, he or she may have difficulty finding everything, because the inspector is only at the home for two to four hours. As home inspectors, we always appreciate an extra set of eyes looking for the issues with us. Ego need not apply, and two heads are always better than one. If you find an issue from the book or something in the home that doesn't look right, point it out to the inspector. Even if you are not quite sure, err on the side of caution—you are undertaking a major investment, and finding potential issues is exceedingly important.

After the home inspection is completed, get the inspection report, read it carefully, and discuss all the findings with your real estate agent. Your inspector is not responsible for telling you what you should or should not do—the inspector's job is merely to find problems. If there are major problems in the home, we recommend that you hire a professional in that particular field to determine how severe the problem may be. Remember that anything in a home can be repaired or replaced, but cost can be an issue. Your real estate agent will know how to proceed.

Scenario #2: You've decided to forgo the professional route and instead do your own home inspection, and you are working with a professional real estate agent.

Plan on taking a few hours to walk through the home, using this book chapter by chapter in the order it is written to assist you in your inspection. Remember that this is not your home (and may not ever be, depending on what you find or how the deal works out) and you must treat it professionally. If you damage anything in the home, whether or not you buy it, you will be responsible for paying for damages. In other words—be careful!

Take your time, study each area as diligently as possible, and cross-reference issues shown in the book with things you see in the home. Use the home inspection checklist found on our site (**www.DoItYourselfHomeInspections.com**), and take as many photos as possible of any problems you find so that you can review them later when writing up your own report after the inspection. After you've had time to review your findings and make some initial decisions about the home, sit down with your real estate agent and go through all of your findings. Your agent will know how to proceed.

Scenario #3: You're purchasing a home that is For Sale by Owner with no real estate agents involved:

First, we strongly recommend hiring a professional real estate agent. As a home buyer, if you do not take all the proper steps, using properly written contracts and negotiation strategies and working carefully with a title company, you will quite possibly have many different problems to deal with in the years to come.

If you have decided to make this purchase on your own, then, as with scenario #2, plan on taking a few hours to walk through the home, using this book chapter by chapter in the order it is written to assist you in your inspection. As stated before, if you break it you pay for it, so be careful and professional. Take notes using the home inspection checklist you grabbed found on our site (**www.DoItYourselfHomeInspections.com**), and snap lots of photos. You'll need these later to study and create a report from, so the more information the better.

After finishing the inspection and mulling over the findings, you will have to decide what you may want to ask the home sellers to repair or replace anything. As a home buyer, based on the home inspection findings you have the right to change your offer, to make requests for some problems to be fixed before the deal closes, or to ask for price concessions. The home sellers have the choice of agreeing to your revised offer or walking away and accepting the next offer in line. This, again, is where a real estate agent's expertise and negotiating skills can come into play.

Now that we have outlined the best ways to work with this book and what to do with your findings, it is time to move forward with the inspection process!

As mentioned before, this book is written chapter by chapter in the order we think works best for the inspection process. By following the book in sequence, you will conduct a thorough inspection of the home from top to bottom in an efficient manner. Use the home inspection checklist from our website and take lots of photos.

At the beginning of each chapter is a breakdown of the must-check areas—the most important things you should look for in that part of the house. These areas are often the big-money issues or safety issues, so check them all carefully.

We have tried our best to show everything we can with high-quality photos and descriptions. While this book will certainly not show you 100 percent of the problems you may find in a home inspection, it does cover an incredibly wide range of them. It is, of course, up to you and your real estate agent to make the final determination about any issues you find, but we have noted any major issues that we feel require an outside professional such as a chimney sweep, electrician, plumber, or HVAC contractor. Pay special attention to these issues, as many times they are safety hazards or expensive repairs. The single most important thing that you should keep in mind as you proceed is that when in doubt, you should consult a professional.

Happy home inspecting!

Chapter 3
Home-Exterior Inspection

When inspecting the exterior of the home, it is especially important to be thorough, because the exterior is one of the most important areas. We have been inspecting homes for over fifteen years and oftentimes find the majority of the problems on the exterior. Furthermore, exterior problems are some of the most expensive to replace and repair.

MUST-CHECK AREAS:

1. WINDOWS—Look at every window, checking for cracked glass, wood rot around the frame, frame damage, and caulking present on only the top side of the window.

2. EXTERIOR DOORS AND SLIDING DOORS—Inspect the exterior of each door. When looking at a French door or sliding door, examine the lower portion of the door very closely. Many of these deteriorate or rot out at five to ten years of age.

3. GRADING—Check that the property grading runs away from the home on all sides. Pay particular attention to the patio and walkways, making sure they have not settled back toward the home.

4. VINYL, METAL, AND WOOD—Examine all the home's siding for any cracks, improper installation, or melted areas caused by barbecue and grill patio fires. Make sure any wooden siding has been scraped and painted and has no exposed wood.

5. DECKING—Decks can pose some of the biggest problems we find in homes today. Look very closely at any deck structures, railings, stairs, flashing between the house and the deck, and the structure below the deck. The majority of problems we find with decks exist because the homeowners tried to save money and did not build them to the proper safety standards.

6. ELECTRICAL OUTLETS—Check all exterior electrical outlets to make sure they are functional and are Ground Fault Circuit Interrupter (GFCI) outlets. GFCI outlets include a reset button or can be connected to a separate GFCI outlet. Each exterior electrical outlet should also be installed with a cover for safety.

7. CRACKED FOUNDATIONS—Look closely for any cracks that have more than one-eighth inch separation and have pushed up, down, or out. Sometimes even a very small, seemingly minor crack can cause water leaks, so check the basement area for potential leaks. We recommend that all foundation cracks be caulked and sealed.

8. CHIMNEYS—Look at the chimney through binoculars, from ground level to the top, checking for straight-line cracks in the bricks, spalling (chipping or scaling) bricks, missing mortar in the joints between bricks, and cracked caps. Chimneys can be very expensive to repair. We recommend that a licensed chimney sweep check every chimney connected to a fireplace and clean its liner.

9. MAIN ELECTRICAL SERVICE—Make sure the electrical service meter is securely fastened to the home. Look up and follow the electrical service wires to the house's service connection, making sure no trees or branches are lying against the wires.

11. ELECTRICAL GROUND ROD—When examining the electrical meter, look on the ground to find a ground rod to which a ground wire should be connected. If you do not see it there, look in the basement. An electrical ground rod may not have been installed and if this is the case you should have one installed if you buy the home

10. WATER FAUCETS—Check each exterior water faucet to confirm it is functional. Make sure each one has a shut-off valve (necessary for the winter months in cold climate areas) in the basement or crawlspace.

11. CRAWL-SPACE VENTS—If the house has a crawl space, check for vents and make sure they are functional, meaning that they open and close.

12. RETAINING WALLS—If the retaining walls are made of wood, make sure they are not rotten and have had deadmen installed. A deadman is a support that runs from the retaining wall back into the ground to give the wall support. If the retaining walls are made of concrete, check for cracking or leaning of the wall. No matter what type of retaining wall the property may contain, check to see if the walls have severe movement or appear to be falling over.

PROBLEMS WITH EXTERIOR SIDING:

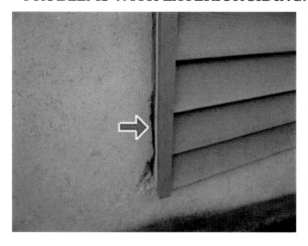

We recommend caulking where the siding and the concrete meet. This will help prevent water and insects from entering the home.

This is a photo of a newer home and all the holes in the wood siding were never properly filled and sealed. This home will most likely need to be completely repainted.

It is common to find wood rot on the wooden siding near a bay window. We recommend re-caulking all seams at least annually and possibly re-staining the siding every three to five years.

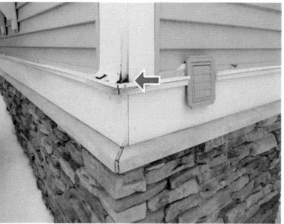

Several newer homes use a type of pressed board exterior siding that if not caulked and sealed properly will rot out quickly.

PROBLEMS WITH EXTERIOR SIDING:

Openings such as these should be filled with concrete or concrete caulk to prevent water from entering behind the stone.

This wood rot just below the roof is caused by the buildup of rainwater or winter ice. We recommend that when you find problems like this you hire a licensed contractor to make all necessary repairs.

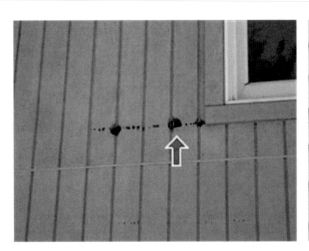

This photo shows where woodpeckers have pecked through the siding and cut into an electrical wire.

Don't leave any wooden areas open to the outside. Any gaps, such as this one next to the gutter, should be caulked to prevent water from leaking into the home.

PROBLEMS WITH EXTERIOR SIDING:

The wooden exterior of this home needs to be scraped and repainted.

This type of overhang looks very nice but often leads to serious water-leak issues at the base of the front entry or where the garage wall and ceiling join to the home.

We frequently find loose stones or stone ledges in this new style of siding.

Loose window ledges are a safety hazard and should be properly secured.

PROBLEMS WITH EXTERIOR BRICK SIDING:

These types of cracks on the exterior of this home are larger than normal. We recommend that you have a licensed contractor make all necessary repairs.

This photo shows a large exterior step-crack. This could be a serious issue, because the wall is actually pushing outward. The step-crack could just be a result of the foundation settling, but we recommend calling a professional to evaluate.

The bricks have separated approximately one inch at the center of the garage door opening. This is difficult to see but the garage door beam was undersized when installed and has allowed the center of the garage entrance support beam to drop. This is a serious issue and will need to be repaired by a licensed contractor.

The brick on the side of this garage has experienced some serious movement. No repairs can be done. The brick must be removed and replaced.

PROBLEMS WITH EXTERIOR BRICK AND WOODEN SIDING:

The brick on the front of this garage is falling and will need to be removed and replaced. Examine any garage that has bricks on its exterior. This is a common problem.

Vegetation growth on the side of a home can destroy the siding or brick. It also prevents you from seeing any exterior damage. The vegetation should be removed after home is purchased.

Cracked bricks above the front left side of the garage door.

This brick has been stained by water leaks. Look for water leaks or stains on both the exterior and the inside of the home. In a situation like this, a gutter should be installed.

This crack was found on the top left corner and top right corner of the garage door's exterior. When you see a crack like this, call a licensed builder—it could be a very costly repair. The center support above the garage door opening may be undersized.

MISCELLANEOUS PROBLEMS WITH EXTERIOR SIDING:

 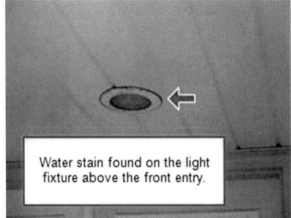

Water stain found on the light fixture above the front entry.

Look closely at the corner support post of any screened-in porches. These are common areas for wood rot. Years ago many homeowners did not use treated lumber when building screened-in porches.

This is a photo of a rusting light fixture. Such rusting generally happens in recessed soffit lighting in porch areas, due to ice backing up on the roof during the winter months.

When you see round holes on the exterior of a home's siding, it generally means that the home has had additional insulation put into the interior and exterior walls. This will help with your home energy bills.

PROBLEMS WITH EXTERIOR WINDOWS AND DOORS:

Both of these windows' tops have been heavily caulked with clear silicone. Such caulking indicates past water leaks. When you see this, inspect the interior of the windows for water stains or current leaks.

A window whose top has been heavily caulked has most likely leaked in the past and you should look closely at the interior of this window.

A steel lintel is a strong section of steel that runs from one end of the window to the other to carry the weight load of the bricks installed on the home's siding. The steel lintel supporting this window opening is rusted and should be replaced.

Check the base of each exterior window and sliding doors for wood rot. It doesn't matter if the home is new or old. We often find wood rot at the base of windows.

PROBLEMS WITH EXTERIOR WINDOWS AND DOORS:

This exterior window has been heavily caulked by a homeowner who does not know how to caulk properly. Look at the window's interior, the interior flooring, and the lower level below the window if possible, since there is a very good chance that this window has leaked into the home.

This new basement window was installed upside down.

Wood rot is commonly found at the base of exterior doors. Look at the interior wall below the door. There is a good chance you will find wood rot in the basement or crawl space.

Look at the exterior of all sliding doors. You will often find that the door frame is rotted.

PROBLEMS WITH EXTERIOR DECKS:

Recommend to have no more than a two-foot cantilever.

A deck should be built with no more than a two-foot overhang or cantilever over the supporting beam. This deck definitely needs another support beam added to provide the proper support and ensure safety.

This deck should not be cantilevered over the main support beam by more than 2 feet. We recommend having additional support added under the cantilevered section for safety.

Lag screws or bolts are needed in the main support beam. Nails are not strong enough to support the weight of a deck full of a group of people.

If at all possible, look under every deck. You never know what type of construction you will find there. The owners of this house wanted a hot tub, so they just added some concrete blocks for additional support. This is not a good idea. The concrete blocks should be replaced with support posts properly installed into the ground by a licensed contractor.

PROBLEMS WITH EXTERIOR DECKS:

Make sure the deck's floor joists are touching the support beams. In this photo, none of the floor joists are actually touching the support beam. If the deck is level, this problem can be repaired by simply adding the proper type of outdoor-treated shims.

This is another photo of a new home in which the person who built the deck missed nailing several of the deck nails into the support beam. This same issue was found on several floor joists.

The underside of the deck has water leaking in different areas.

This support beam has been nailed to the deck post. We recommend that it also be lag-screwed or bolted to the post. Lag screws and bolts are designed to withstand heavy weight loads. Their absence here presents a possible safety hazard.

This is a photo of the underside of a covered deck. Luckily, it was raining at the time of the inspection, and we were able to determine that the underside of the deck was leaking water. This problem is not easy to find unless you see water stains or it is currently raining.

DECKS, LEDGER BOARDS, FLOOR JOISTS, AND JOIST HANGERS:

This photo shows deck floor joists with properly installed joist hangers. Make sure that the proper size joist hanger was used and the proper number of nails was used to install each joist hanger.

This photo shows deck flashing that has been properly installed. Deck flashing is used to prevent water from entering the home where the deck and the home meet.

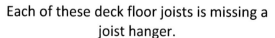

Each of these deck floor joists is missing a joist hanger.

This is a photo of a deck ledger board not lag-screwed to the house. It is critical that the deck be installed properly to ensure the safety of you, your family, and your guests.

DECK RAILINGS, STAIRS, AND PROBLEM AREAS:

Properly installed deck railings.

Three stair stringers

Support post

Properly installed deck stairs

These deck spindles and railings were properly installed: the railings are thirty-six inches tall and the spindles are four inches apart.

These deck stairs were properly installed. There are outside stair stringers on each side and one in the center and the base of the staircase has a support post running into the ground.

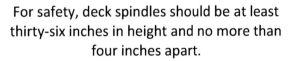

For safety, deck spindles should be at least thirty-six inches in height and no more than four inches apart.

These deck stairs need a third stringer added for proper support. Stringers are the two-inch by 12-inch boards on the outside of the deck stairs.

PROBLEMS WITH EXTERIOR DECK STAIRS AND RAILINGS:

These deck stairs do not have railings. The lack of railings poses a safety hazard.

These deck railings look visually appealing, but they should be able to hold a person if leaning up against them. This railing system will need to be repaired and be able to withstand the proper weight against it.

We recommend that deck railings be installed on the staircase for safety.

The deck stairs have settled and should be repaired.

These deck stairs have settled, and the support post for the staircase has rotted. The staircase should be repaired by a licensed contractor.

PROBLEMS WITH DRIVEWAYS AND WALKWAYS:

This is an example of a driveway cracking and settling.

Driveway or walkway settling can pose a safety hazard that may cause people to trip and fall.

This problem is sometimes difficult to find, but because we did the inspection while it was raining we saw that sand was washing out from under the driveway. This washing away, if not corrected, will eventually cause the driveway to settle and crack.

This is a brand-new home at which the concrete was poured incorrectly and slopes back toward the garage. This slope allows water to flow back into the garage.

PROBLEMS WITH PORCHES AND PATIOS:

The front porch of this home has settled and moved the corner support post. Sometimes you may not notice problems like this until you step away from the home and look at it from a few feet away.

This front porch post has rotted. Porches are common areas for wood rot.

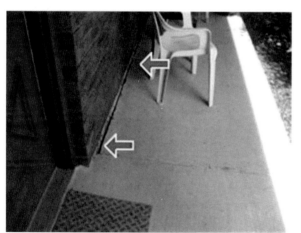

This front porch has pulled away from the home, allowing rainwater to run back toward the home. Check the basement closely for water leaks or damaged wood.

The front porch in this photo has pulled away from the home. The problem can be repaired by mud jacking, but that is very expensive. Mud jacking is a process in which concrete is pumped underneath a foundation or a slab of concrete to lift it into the correct position.

PROBLEMS WITH PORCHES AND PATIOS:

This concrete patio has settled back toward the home, allowing rainwater to run back toward the home. Check the basement closely for water leaks or damaged wood.

This concrete patio was poured incorrectly, with the slope going back toward the home. This slope can cause serious water leaks in the home. Look closely around the interior of the door.

Check to see if the front porch has settled back toward the home. If it has, there is a good chance water has leaked into the basement. This front porch has dropped approximately two inches sloping back toward the home.

In this photo the siding has been caulked where it meets the porch concrete. Caulking is generally a sign of a past water leak. Look for water stains or wood rot in the basement or crawl space directly below this area.

PROBLEMS WITH PORCHES AND PATIOS:

The center of this front porch overhang has dropped due to wood rot and will need to be repaired.

This home is less than two years old, and none of the front porch's concrete pillar caps were properly secured to the base.

This is a flip home. Some flip homes are finished by professionals and are put together perfectly, but others, like this one, have construction shortcomings that pose safety hazards.

This front porch has shifted, causing the brick to fall off the porch. We recommend having this problem repaired by a licensed contractor.

EXTERIOR FOUNDATION CRACKS:

Cracks in the home's foundation generally don't cause structural issues, but you should look for related water leaks in the basement. We recommend that every crack be caulked and sealed to help prevent further issues.

This is a wall crack commonly found on the exterior of older block-foundation homes. This particular crack is not causing any structural concerns. If you are not comfortable with your findings, call a professional home inspector. We still advise that every one of these cracks is sealed to help prevent water leaks.

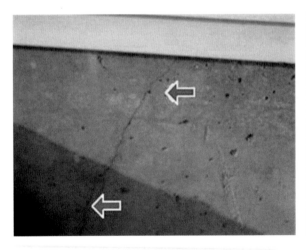

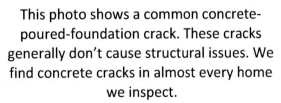

This photo shows a common concrete-poured-foundation crack. These cracks generally don't cause structural issues. We find concrete cracks in almost every home we inspect.

Here we see serious foundation movement on the back side of a garage. This should be checked and repaired by a licensed professional.

EXTERIOR FOUNDATION CRACKS:

This home has a serious exterior foundation crack; the foundation is pushing outward on one side and should be checked by a professional.

Large exterior foundation cracks should be checked by a professional. This foundation has moved approximately one inch. This is a serious concern.

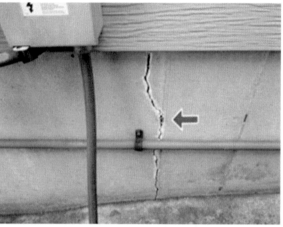

The foundation of this home has shifted approximately two inches or more. This home is located near a lake and was originally built as a cottage. People are now buying these homes and wanting to rebuild them, but in many cases the foundations do not hold up. This is a serious problem.

This foundation is a little larger than we would consider acceptable. When you see a crack like this one call a professional to check it. You should also check for water leaks or other problems on the other side of the crack in the basement or crawl space. A crack like this will most likely need to be professionally sealed.

PROBLEMS WITH RETAINING WALLS:

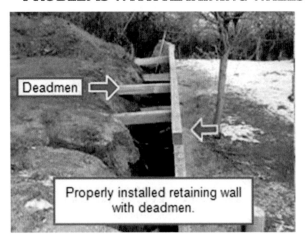

In this photo you can see the proper installation of deadmen into the ground to hold up the wall in the proper position.

This retaining wall is falling over and has moved approximately 1 ½ feet. It appears to have been installed properly using deadmen for support, however the deadmen are fake which has allowed the wall to move. This home is only five years old.

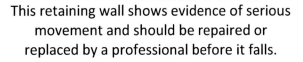

This retaining wall shows evidence of serious movement and should be repaired or replaced by a professional before it falls.

This retaining wall is missing steps for exiting the egressed basement window. We recommend having steps installed for exiting in case of an emergency.

PROBLEMS WITH LANDSCAPE GRADING:

This backyard's slope toward the home could cause serious water troubles. This home has a high probability of water leaking into the basement.

This side yard should slope away from the home. The current grading is sending water toward the home, which can allow water to leak into the basement.

This driveway should be sloped away from the home. The current slope can cause water to leak into the basement and it is also a good reason why homeowners install heavy caulk where the home and the driveway meet.

This new home was not graded properly. Water has been running down the side of the home, into the sliding door, and into the home.

LANDSCAPE GRADING PROBLEMS:

This walkway should be sloped away from the home, not toward it. The current slope can cause water to run toward the home and leak into the basement.

This is a photo of poor drainage. We recommend that you look under any decks to make sure water is running away from the home. Water not running in the proper direction can cause serious problems.

This photo shows poor grading on the exterior of a home. We recommend a 10 percent slope away from the home to help keep water out of the basement.

This is another example of poor grading on the exterior of a home. Again, a 10 percent slope away from the home is appropriate.

PROBLEMS WITH EXTERIOR TREES:

All trees should be cut back from the rooftops. Trees can damage the roof and decrease the life expectancy of the shingles.

All trees should be cut back from the siding. Having trees too close to the home prevents it from drying out.

All trees should be cut back from the roof and siding.

EXTERIOR ELECTRICAL METERS PROPERLY INSTALLED:

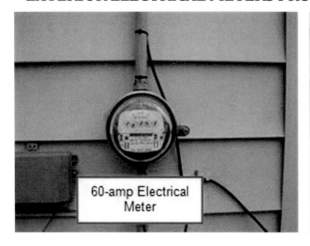

This is a properly installed 60-amp electrical meter, found in older homes.

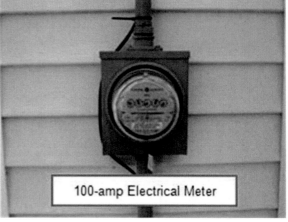

This is a 100-amp electrical meter, generally found in small homes or condominiums today.

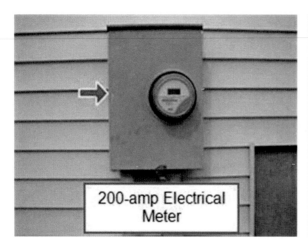

This photo shows a 200-amp electrical meter, found in the majority of new homes today.

This is a photo of a 100-amp electrical meter with a main disconnect on the exterior of the home.

PROBLEMS WITH EXTERIOR ELECTRICAL SERVICE POLES, AND METERS:

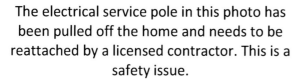

The electrical service pole in this photo has been pulled off the home and needs to be reattached by a licensed contractor. This is a safety issue.

This electrical service pole is bent to the left, which could pose a safety hazard. The pole should be repaired by a licensed electrician.

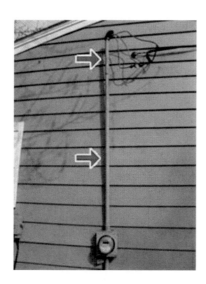

This electrical service pole is loose and needs to be secured to the home by a licensed contractor.

The electrical meter on the exterior of this home is loose and should be secured by a licensed contractor.

PROBLEMS WITH EXTERIOR ELECTRICAL SERVICE POLES, METERS, AND GROUND WIRES:

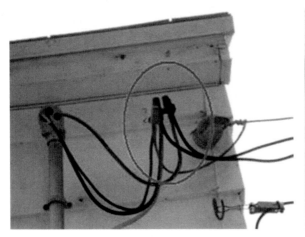

Ground rod properly installed

Exterior electrical service wires should not be wired using interior wire nuts. An electrician should be called to make any necessary repairs.

When looking at the electrical meter on the exterior of the home, look down at the ground to locate a ground rod with a connected ground wire. Sometimes the ground rod is located in the basement instead. Some older homes will not have one at all.

The electrical service cap is cracked and should be replaced by a licensed contractor.

When inspecting the roof, check the electrical service pole's rubber boot for cracks. Such cracks could cause a serious water leak.

EXTERIOR ELECTRICAL WIRES AND GAS METERS:

All wires that run from the home to the exterior must be run in a metal conduit covering to protect the wire. Any other installation may pose a safety hazard.

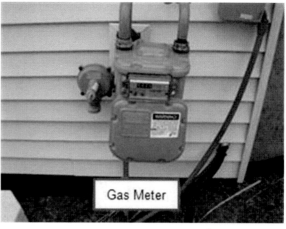

This photo shows a properly installed gas meter.

This is an exterior GFCI outlet with a cover and a reset button.

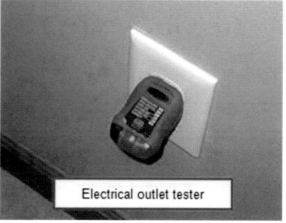

This photo demonstrates the use of a tool called an electrical outlet tester. The large button near the outlet end of the tester, when pushed, will test if the outlet is GFCI-protected.

EXTERIOR ELECTRICAL OUTLETS:

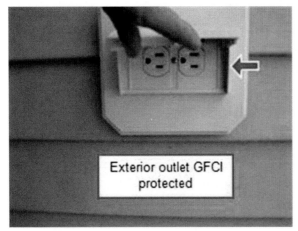

This exterior electrical outlet may still be GFCI-protected even though it does not have a reset button. The best way to test this outlet is to use an electrical outlet tester. The tester will trip the reset button on the associated GFCI outlet which is probably located in the garage.

This is a photo of a GFCI-protected outlet with a reset button. Every time you trip an outlet you should search for the reset outlet or breaker on the electrical panel until you find it. You would hate to shut off the homeowner's garage refrigerator or freezer without anyone knowing.

All exterior outlets should be tested with an electrical outlet tester to determine if they are GFCI-protected. This outlet could have been GFCI-protected to another outlet or to a GFCI breaker in the main panel. All exterior outlets should be installed with covers over them.

MISCELLANEOUS:

Whole House Generator

When you are inspecting the electrical on the exterior of the home, make sure trees are not touching the main service wires. If they are the trees should be cut back.

This photo is of a whole house generator. If you a buying a home with this type of unit, you should have a professional come out and inspect it. These units can be anywhere from $3,000 to over $10,000 depending on the size.

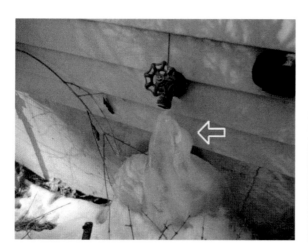

This water faucet is dripping and can eventually freeze up the water line inside the home.

We recommend disconnecting all water faucets from hoses during the winter.

RADON SYSTEM:

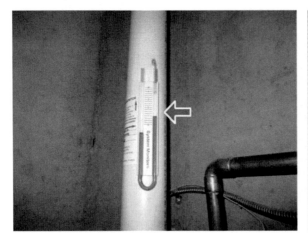

This photo shows a radon fan gauge showing you that the unit is operating. If the gauge were at the same height the fan would not be operating.

This photo shows a radon system on the exterior of the home.

Make sure you caulk around all the different lines coming out of your home, including plumbing, electrical, heating vents, sprinkler systems and any others.

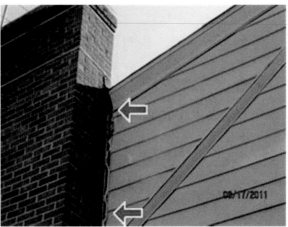

The chimney has moved away from the home several inches, as evidenced by the fact that it has been caulked multiple times.

Chapter 4
Garage Inspection

Although the garage is a relatively minor part of a home inspection, it is amazing how many times we have found costly problems in it. Inspect the entire garage carefully.

MUST-CHECK AREAS:

1. GARAGE DOOR—Check the garage door for damage. If the garage door does not have an electronic opener, make sure it opens and closes.

2. GARAGE DOOR OPENER—Make sure the garage door opener and the auto reverse operate properly. When inspecting the auto reverse function for a garage door, you may notice that the homeowner has installed the auto reverse electronic eyes on the top of the door. This is not a safe installation.

3. INSIDE GARAGE WALLS—Check for water stains on the wall where the house and the garage meet. Even in new houses, it is common to find water stains and wood rot directly behind garage-front walls that have been half bricked on the exterior.

4. FIRE SAFETY OF INTERIOR GARAGE WALLS AND ENTRY DOOR—Check the interior walls of the garage where they meet the house for fire safety, and make sure that the door leading into the home from the garage is a proper one-hour, fire-safe solid wood or metal door. Check that fire-rated drywall has been installed where the home and the garage meet. Fire-safe drywall is generally five-eighths-inch thick. Check that the hatch covers in the ceiling are made of a fire-rated material. Check with your local building inspector for the proper codes.

5. GARAGE OUTLETS—Ensure that all electrical outlets are GFCI outlets and are functional.

6. SIDE GARAGE DOOR—Check each side door in the garage to make sure that its threshold is not rotted and that the door is operational.

7. GARAGE CEILINGS—Garage ceilings, especially where the home and the garage meet, are common places for water leaks to occur. Using a flashlight, look for water stains and for places where the ceiling has been repaired or repainted. You should also look for water stains in the attic of the garage.

8. GARAGE WINDOWS—Garage windows commonly have water leaks. Even if items are stored in front of them, do your best to look behind and under the windows.

PROBLEMS WITH GARAGE DOORS AND OPENERS:

This garage door opener has been properly installed and wired to a direct, dedicated outlet.

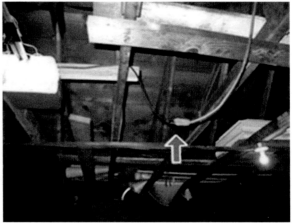

This garage door opener has been wired using an extension cord. We recommend that garage door openers instead be wired to a direct, dedicated outlet.

Check both sides—interior and exterior—of a garage door for damage.

This photo is included, because many people don't know how to operate these older Sears garage door opener buttons. To open or close this garage door, you have to push both buttons at the same time.

PROBLEMS WITH GARAGE DOORS AND OPENERS:

This garage door opener's spring is broken. We recommend having a professional repair garage doors. A broken garage door can be a serious safety hazard.

This electronic garage door eye has been properly installed between four inches and six inches off the ground.

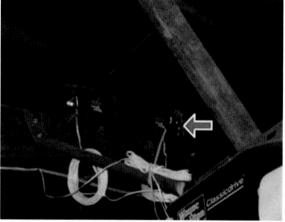

As a safety precaution, the electronic eyes should be installed between four inches and six inches off the ground.

These garage door safety sensors have been attached to the ceiling of a garage, which poses a safety hazard.

PROBLEMS WITH GARAGE CEILINGS:

Here we see heavy ice buildup where the house and the garage meet. When you see this, look closely at the floor and wall of both the garage and the home.

This water stain is located on the ceiling near where the house and the garage meet, a common place for water stains to occur. If you find a stain like this, look for additional water stains or damage in the garage attic and on the house side of the garage wall.

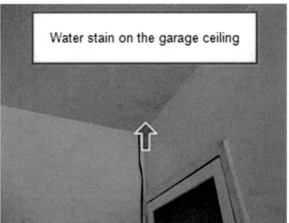

Water stain on the garage ceiling

This photo also shows water stains on the garage ceiling near where the house and the garage meet.

PROBLEMS WITH GARAGE ATTICS:

The garage wall has moved 6-inches to the left

Water stains and current water leaks in the garage

Look closely at every wall in the garage. This wall has actually shifted 6 inches and will need to be repaired.

In this photo, we see a water stain in the garage attic where the house and the garage meet.

PROBLEMS WITH GARAGE STRUCTURES:

The arrows in this photo are pointing to a cable that has been installed to provide additional support to the garage. The garage is most likely leaning to one side or the other, which may be cause for concern.

When you inspect a garage, always look closely at the sill plate. The sill plate is the two-by-four that lies on the concrete; the two-by-four studs for the walls are built on top of the sill plate. Wood rot and termites are frequently found in the sills of a garage.

PROBLEMS WITH GARAGE FIRE SAFETY WALLS, DOORS, AND ATTIC ENTRANCES:

Properly installed

We recommend to install a one hour rated fire door

This photo shows a one-hour fire-safe metal door leading from the garage into the house.

People often install doors like these leading to the garage because they are visually appealing; however a one hour fire door should instead be a solid steel door with no windows.

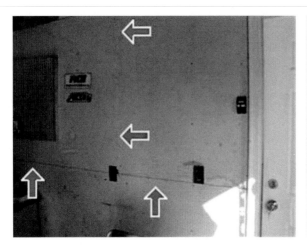

The wall that joins the home and the garage was installed with five-eights-inch fire-barrier drywall, but for the wall to be complete the drywall lines must also be taped and mudded.

Houses should not have gable vents in the garage, because it becomes a fire hazard. This opening should be sealed with five-eights-inch fire-barrier drywall.

MISCELLANEOUS GARAGE PROBLEMS:

Heat vents can be particularly dangerous when installed inside a garage because of the possibility of carbon monoxide getting into the home.

The step leading into the home from the garage was not built to current local standards since it is an older home. You should be cautious about starting your automobile in the garage because of the chance of carbon monoxide flowing back into your home.

GARAGE ELECTRICAL OUTLETS, WIRES, AND LIGHT FIXTURES

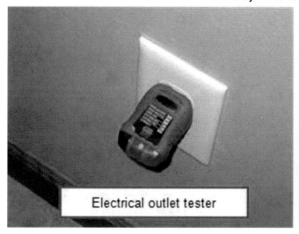

Electrical outlet tester

GFCI electrical outlet - Ground fault circuit interrupter

This is an electrical outlet tester with a GFCI test trip button. When you push the trip button (the large black one on the outlet end of the tester), the outlet's power should turn off.

All garage outlets should be GFCI-protected for safety. Even if the outlet does not have a reset button like in the picture above, it may be GFCI-protected. One of the only ways you can test it is to use an electrical outlet tester.

Chapter 5
Roof Inspection

For safety reasons we do not recommend that any home buyer walks on the roof. You should bring a ladder and look at the roof from as many different sides as possible without walking on the roof. We recommend that you bring a set of high-powered binoculars—these will help you in examining two-story roofs from a distance. Safety is very important.

MUST-CHECK AREAS:

1. SHINGLES—Look at the shingles to determine their approximate remaining life. Look for curling shingles, loss of roof shingle granules, nail pops, damaged shingles, caulked valleys, and any other visible problems. Several kinds of roofing materials are used on houses. If you do not understand the roofing material on the home you are inspecting you should contact a professional for help.

2. NEW SHINGLES—Even if you were told the shingles are new and have been installed less than a year ago, you should still look at them, especially watching out for nail pops. We have found several houses that each had hundreds of nail pops, and the affected shingles must be replaced. Regardless of type or age, the roof should always be inspected.

3. ROOF VALLEY—Three types of roof valleys are commonly in use today: closed valley, metal valley and open valley. We have found very few problems with closed valleys, except closed valleys that have been caulked. Such caulking generally tells us the valley has leaked in the past and has been patched or repaired. In our opinion, the metal valley is the best way to go. If installed properly, it generally doesn't have problems. Open valleys should be examined closely. We find the rolled roofing associated with open valleys typically cracks or deteriorates ten to fifteen years after installation.

4. ROOF VENTILATION—There are four types of roof ventilation: roof vents, ridge vents, soffit vents, and gable vents. Most homes built today have soffit vents and either ridge vents or roof vents. Older homes may contain any combination of vent types, since there were not many standards.

5. PLUMBING VENT PIPE BOOT COVERS—Examine the rubber vent pipe boot covers, checking for cracks. Normally, after approximately ten years the rubber boot starts cracking and will need to be replaced. If not replaced, it can cause water leaks.

6. CHIMNEY FLASHING—Look at the chimney flashing to make sure it is properly installed and to determine if it needs to be re-caulked. If the roof is safely accessible, we recommend checking the flashing and possibly re-caulking it twice a year.

7. GUTTERS—Make sure all the gutters are clean and have downspout diverters running the water away from the home. When walking around the home, look up at all of the gutters to check for rusted areas that are or will be leaking water. Pay particular attention to the corners of the house.

8. MULTIPLE LAYERS OF SHINGLES—Determining how many layers of shingles are on the roof may be difficult. Look at the drip edge and try to count the layers. If the drip edge is a C channel (we have photos of these in the book), there will be multiple layers. A normal drip edge will have only one layer. Another way to determine how many layers of shingles is to go into the attic and look at the number of nails that have been installed.

9. ROOFING MATERIALS

A. ASPHALT ROOFING SHINGLES—Asphalt shingles are the most commonly used material for residential roofs in the United States. They are durable, easy to install, and moderately priced.

B. WOOD—Wooden roofing products are available in two basic forms: wooden shingles and wooden shakes. Shingles are produced by sawing wood into long tapered shapes; shakes are produced by splitting wood into long tapered shapes. Sawing produces a more uniformly shaped and relatively smooth surface. Splitting produces a rough, highly textured appearance. Wooden shingles and shakes tend to be expensive to purchase and install.

C. METAL—Metallic-coated steel, copper, aluminum, and stainless steel are some metals commonly used for roofing. Galvanized (zinc-coated) steel is the most common coated metal used for roofing. Metal roofs are relatively lightweight and vary greatly in price depending on the type of metal.

D. TILE—Clay, concrete, and fiber cement are the three most common materials used in roof tiles. Of the three, clay tiles are the most expensive. Tile roofs have a class-A fire rating and create a pleasing, textured look. Tile roofs are difficult and time-consuming to install.

E. SLATE—Slate is probably the most durable roofing material of all. In fact, the slate itself will last forever. The fasteners and flashings that hold the slates to the roof are the limiting factor in the life of a slate roof. But if proper fasteners and flashing are used and the installation is done carefully, a slate roof has a life span of at least a hundred years.

PROBLEMS WITH ASPHALT SHINGLES:

This photo shows properly installed roof shingles.

These shingles are deteriorating due to age. They are starting to bubble up in various areas.

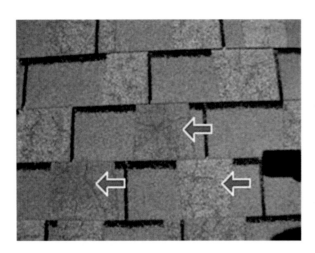

These shingles have cracked due to age. The severity of the cracks determines the remaining life of the shingles. These shingles have approximately five or fewer years of life remaining.

These shingles are losing excessive amounts of granules. This problem is sometimes viewable only from on top of the roof or from a ladder. Look at the shingles as closely as you can.

PROBLEMS WITH ASPHALT SHINGLES:

New shingles were installed on only one half of the roof. In this particular case the backside of the roof shingles are still functional but they are still older.

Shingles become damaged like these because of the incredible amount of heat that builds up in the attic as a result of poor attic ventilation. The shingles need to be replaced, and proper ventilation must be installed in the attic to prevent recurrence of the problem.

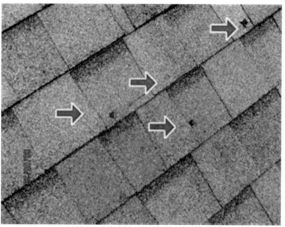

The little black spots on these shingles are granular pitting. The severity of the pitting will determine the remaining life of the shingles. When you see something like this you are nearing the end of the shingles' useful life.

These asphalt shingles have nail pops. This problem can be seen only by getting on top of the roof. If you find only a couple nail pops, you can just repair them. If you find several, it is time to call in a professional roofer—there is a good chance the shingles will have to be replaced.

PROBLEMS WITH ASPHALT SHINGLES:

This is a properly installed ridge shingle placed on top of a ridge vent.

This roof ridge was finished by cutting the roof shingles to fit over the ridge. The roof is not defective, but we recommend that the best way to roof a ridge is to install ridge and hip shingles (specially designed singles for the ridge and hip areas).

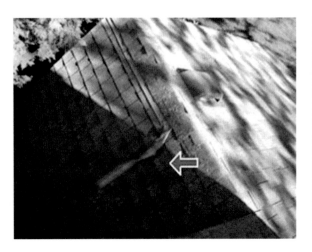

The metal strip hanging from the ridge is a zinc strip that helps keep the shingles clear of moss and mold. As it rains, the water hits the zinc strip and washes off the roof.

When you see a gable roof like this hanging over another roof, you should look below the overhang to see if there are any openings to the attic. If you find any openings, they should be covered or sealed.

PROBLEMS WITH ASPHALT SHINGLES:

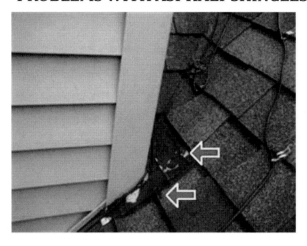

A roof area like this commonly experiences ice buildup in the winter months. The roof in this photo also contains a heat wire for ice. Look very closely below this roof area for any water leaks in the home.

Debris should be cleared from the shingles—not allowed to build up as has happened on this roof.

We found several shingles missing from this roof. In this case, check several shingle tabs to see if they are sticking down properly. These shingles had to be removed and new shingles installed.

These shingles are deteriorating due to age. Shingles that look like this need to be replaced. Most states allow up to two layers of shingles, but we recommend removing all the old shingles before installing the new ones.

PROBLEMS WITH ASPHALT SHINGLES:

The shingles on this home were in excellent condition, except for those located one foot above the perimeter near the gutters. When you look closely at them, you can see that the tar paper underneath the shingles is completely gone and the wood is visible. This is not good; call a professional roofer.

This roof appears very good when you look at it from the ground, but once you get on the roof you realize how much the shingles have deteriorated and how many granules have fallen off. These shingles will need to be replaced within two to three years.

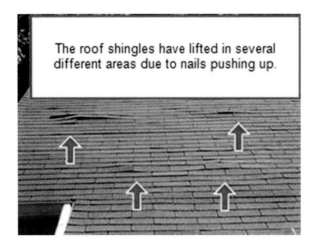

The roof shingles have lifted in several different areas due to nails pushing up.

These roof shingles are most likely lifting up because of nails pops, in which case there is a good chance the shingles will need to be replaced.

When you are looking at the roof, make sure all the nail heads are covered with caulk to help prevent roof leaks. This oversight is commonly found with new roofs but is also inexpensive to repair.

PROBLEMS WITH ROLLED ASPHALT AND RUBBER ROOFING:

Fabricated in the same way as asphalt shingles, rolled roofing is generally installed on roofs that have less than a 2:12 pitch. We typically find the life of the product to be approximately ten years.

This is a photo of rolled roofing on a flat or low-pitched roof of less than 2:12 pitch.

The rolled roofing here is in very poor condition and will need to be replaced.

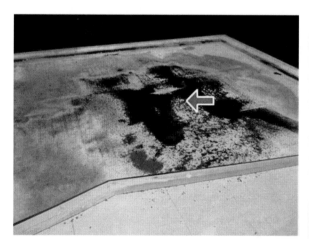

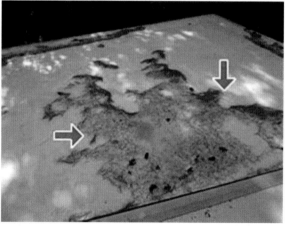

This is a photo of a flat roof with a large puddle of water. We recommend hiring a professional to inspect any flat roof.

This is a photo of another flat roof with a large puddle of water. We recommend hiring a professional to inspect any flat roof.

PROBLEMS WITH ROLLED ASPHALT AND RUBBER ROOFING:

Rolled rubber roofing is generally found on flat roofs. It is an excellent product and lasts approximately twenty to twenty-five years.

This rolled rubber roofing is cracking. If you see something like this, we recommend hiring a roofing expert to inspect it. The roof is most likely nearing the end of its life.

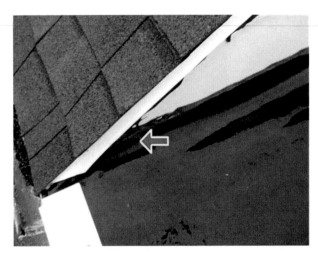

This rubber roofing was improperly installed where it connects to the home and needs to be repaired.

The rolled roofing has been repaired over the garage

This rolled roofing has been repaired with screws and washers. The repair will not last long, and we recommend having it repaired by a licensed roofer.

WOODEN CEDAR SHAKE SHINGLES, TERRA COTTA CLAY TILES, AND SLATE SHINGLES:

Wooden cedar shake shingles

Terra cotta clay tiles

Slate shingles

METAL ROOFING:

Metal roofing generally comes in two types: flat seam or standing seam. A standing-seam metal roof generally lasts seventy-five to one hundred years if properly maintained with periodic scraping and rust-resistant paint.

WOODEN SHAKE ROOF:

These wooden shake shingles are covered in moss. We recommend having a professional roofer either clean or replace this roofing.

BUILT-UP ROOFING:

This is a photo of a built-up roof with no issues. Built-up roofs are uncommon in today's homebuilding, so if you do not completely understand them we recommend you hire a licensed professional.

This is a photo of a built-up roof. If you see a roof like this, you should call either a professional home inspector or a roofer who specializes in this type of roof.

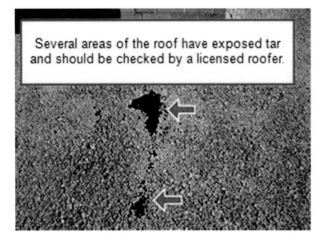

Several areas of the roof have exposed tar and should be checked by a licensed roofer.

If you purchase a home that has a built-up roof, plan on walking the roof at least twice a year to clear off debris and to cover any exposed areas with gravel.

TYPES OF ROOF VALLEYS:

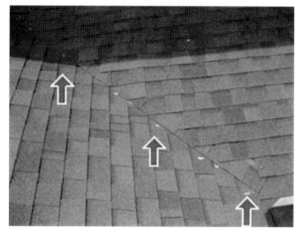

This is an example of a closed valley, the type of roof valley most commonly used today.

Open metal valley

This is a butterfly valley. We don't find many issues with this type of valley, but many roofers do not like to install them.

PROBLEMS WITH ROOF VALLEYS:

Several years ago open valleys were commonly installed but were known to last only approximately half as long as the shingles. This open valley has been heavily tarred due to a possible water leak or a retreating valley. This valley has limited life remaining.

Both of these closed valleys have been caulked, generally indicating a leak.

This deteriorating open valley should be repaired or replaced.

This valley has not been properly installed. It was probably installed by a homeowner who tried to save money by roofing his or her own home. We recommend that this be repaired by a licensed roofing contractor.

PROBLEMS WITH ROOF VALLEYS:

Both of these valleys have been heavily tarred, which will work as only a temporary bandage. We recommend having the valleys replaced by a professional roofer.

Look closely at all roof valleys. It is common to find them in poor condition. Always have them repaired or replaced by a professional roofer.

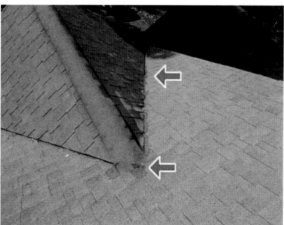

This is a photo of a roof valley with nails placed directly into its center. This installation is incorrect and will cause water leaks. The roof should probably be replaced.

This roof valley has been heavily caulked, and roof shingle granules have been added to it. This repair was most likely in response to a water leak.

ROOF CHIMNEY SADDLES (CRICKETS):

This is a properly installed roof chimney saddle, also known as a cricket.

This is a photo of a chimney with no saddle (cricket) installed. A chimney saddle (cricket) is important, because it sends water away from the chimney, which helps prevent water leaks.

This is a very nicely installed chimney saddle (cricket). But why are both valleys heavily caulked? Such caulking generally indicates past water leaks.

One of the most common roof problems is an improperly flashed chimney.

MULTIPLE LAYERS OF SHINGLES ON THE ROOF:

 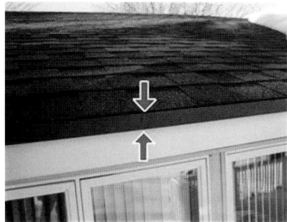

The white area that the arrows are pointing to is a drip edge. A white drip edge usually—but not always—indicates that there is only one layer of shingles. Look closely at the shingles and the roof's edge to make your best, educated assessment.

The brown area directly under the shingles is called a C-channel. When you see one of these directly below your shingles, there is a very good chance the roof has two layers of shingles. If the C-channel is much wider than this, the roof may have three or more layers of shingles.

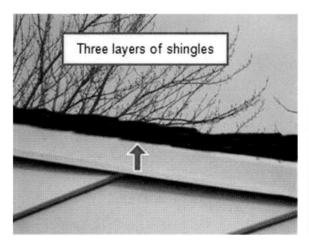
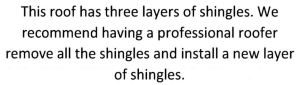
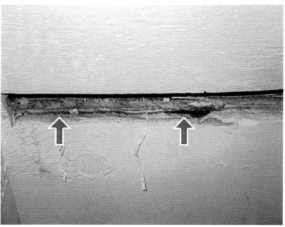

This roof has three layers of shingles. We recommend having a professional roofer remove all the shingles and install a new layer of shingles.

You may need to go up to the attic to determine how many layers of shingles are on a roof. This roof has three layers of shingles and two layers of roof boards, so is extremely overloaded.

PROPERLY INSTALLED ROOF VENTILATION:

Roof vents are located on top of the roof and the number of them depends on the size of the roof.

A ridge vent is one continuous vent that runs along the roof ridge.

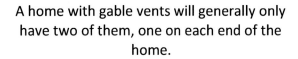

A home with gable vents will generally only have two of them, one on each end of the home.

A turbine vent is a passive ventilation device. This vent works off the air flow in the attic and is normally found on metal roofs.

PROBLEMS WITH ROOF SKYLIGHTS:

Skylights add light and beauty to a home but are subject to water leaks and allow heat and sunlight to enter the home. Look closely around the exterior perimeter of any skylight for heavy caulking that may have been added in response to water leaks.

When examining skylights, look closely to see if they have been heavily caulked, which often indicates a past water leak. Also look at the window itself to see if it is foggy, which may indicate a broken thermal seal.

PROBLEMS WITH SOFFIT VENTS:

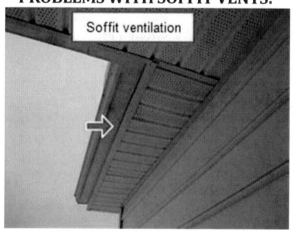

Soffit ventilation

This is a photo of a type of soffit venting currently used around the exterior of a home.

This is a slightly older type of soffit vent.

PROBLEMS WITH SOFFIT VENTS:

Evidence of past ice back up on the front of the home

This photo is of a soffit vent. Look closely at all soffit vents to make sure when the home was painted none of the soffits were plugged with paint. Plugged soffit vents can impair attic ventilation in the extreme temperatures of both summer and winter months.

This photo indicates that this area of the roof has experienced ice backup during the winter months and water flowed back into the soffit area.

PROBLEMS WITH ROOF GUTTERS:

This photo shows that the downspout diverter is missing. A downspout diverter directs water away from the foundation of the home.

These gutters need to be cleaned.

PROBLEMS WITH ROOF GUTTERS:

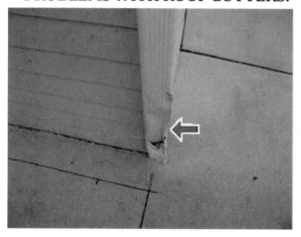

This downspout is damaged and the downspout diverter, which would direct water away from the home's foundation, is missing.

This gutter is missing its end cap.

PROPERLY INSTALLED ROOF/ATTIC VENTILATION:

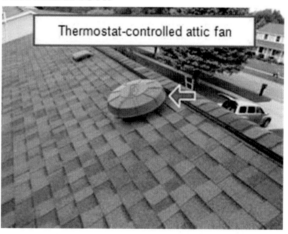

A thermostat-controlled attic vent is generally used on homes in which no other type of ventilation will operate properly. The unit is wired to the home's electrical system and runs automatically with a thermostat control for hot and cold. These vents work very well but can be a somewhat loud.

This is another view of a thermostat-controlled attic fan. These vents can significantly improve a home's roof ventilation system.

ROOF ICE BACKUP:

Water appears to be backing up and entering the home from this roof area.

If you are inspecting a home during winter and you see this type of ice backup, enter the home and check the interior wall directly near and below the ice backup.

In this photo the ice backup on the siding indicates that ice and water is building up on the roof and flowing down through the roof, into the soffit area of the attic, then back out to the exterior of the home. Wood rot may be occurring in the soffit area of the roof, which is difficult to view from most attics.

Heavy ice back up in several different areas.

Ice jamming is a serious concern. It normally happens because of poor ventilation and insulation in the attic.

Chapter 6
Chimney Inspection

Many homes in the United States use fireplaces as their primary or secondary heat source. It is important that items such as flues and chimneys operate properly and are inspected and cleaned on a regular basis depending on their usage. Every fireplace, and every fossil-fuel-burning appliance for that matter, must have a separate chimney flue. The exception is that a furnace and a water heater can share a flue. The water heater flue stove pipe enters above the heating plant's flue.

MUST-CHECK AREAS:

1. CHIMNEY HEIGHT—Chimneys must extend two feet higher than any portion of the roof or any structure within ten feet but can be no more than three feet above the point where the chimney exits the roof.

2. BRICK CHIMNEYS—A chimney with a one-brick thickness and that does not have a flue liner is a fire hazard. A two-brick thick chimney without a flue liner is acceptable as long the chimney is in good condition. Metal flues for gas appliances should always have caps. We recommend adding metal caps over tile chimney liners to prevent animals and birds from nesting.

3. CHIMNEY CRACKS—Look at the brick of the chimney and any fireplace for any crack that runs in a straight line up through three or four layers of brick. Such cracks are sometimes caused by a past chimney fire. We recommend having your chimney and fireplace liners cleaned and inspected by a professional before purchasing the home. This cleaning can save you hundreds or even thousands of dollars.

4. CHIMNEY CROWNS—Chimney crowns should be installed to prevent water from seeping inside the bricks and causing damage. Chimney crowns can be either metal or concrete.

5. SPALLING BRICKS—Spalling occurs when water gets into the bricks and freezes, causing the surface of the brick to flake off. This generally happens when the chimney cap is failing.

6. TUCK POINTING—Tuck pointing is the process of repairing mortar that is falling out from between the bricks.

PROBLEMS WITH CHIMNEYS:

This photo shows a properly installed chimney cap.

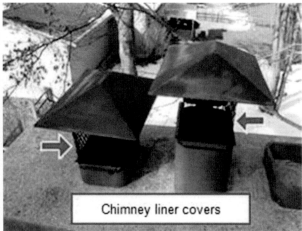

Metal chimney liner covers help keep chimney liners clear of debris and animals.

This chimney has a straight-line crack, which may be a sign of a past chimney fire. We recommend that a licensed chimney sweep inspect the chimney.

This photo shows chimney-brick spalling and loose mortar joints. These should be repaired by a licensed chimney sweep.

PROBLEMS WITH CHIMNEYS:

This chimney needs to have approximately eight layers of bricks replaced and a new chimney cap installed.

A straight-line chimney crack generally means that a chimney fire has occurred. When you see a straight-line crack, hire a licensed chimney sweep to inspect the entire chimney. Such cracks pose a safety hazard.

This chimney cap is cracked in several places and needs to be replaced. If the cap is not replaced, eventually the bricks will deteriorate.

This photo shows a deteriorating roof chimney cap that needs to be replaced.

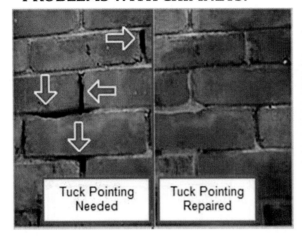

PROBLEMS WITH CHIMNEYS:

The before and after photos demonstrate the effect of tuck pointing, in which concrete is filled in between the chimney's bricks.

Here we see chimney bricks that need tuck pointing to be repaired.

This chimney cap is deteriorating. A new cap should be installed.

These chimney bricks need to be tuck pointed.

PROBLEMS WITH CHIMNEYS:

Chimney liner inspection is very important, because chimney liners carry exhaust from fireplaces, furnaces, and water heaters. A dirty chimney liner is one of the leading causes of house fires today. We recommend that every fireplace liner be cleaned and inspected by professional, licensed chimney sweep.

This chimney carries exhaust from either a furnace or a hot water heater rather than a fireplace, but it should still have a liner. We recommend having a new metal liner installed by a licensed professional.

This chimney has a metal liner and a metal cap, but you should examine the top of it to see if it has rusted or if it needs to be re-caulked.

These chimney tiles are damaged and should be replaced by a licensed chimney sweep.

This chimney liner is full of creosote and poses a fire hazard. It needs to be cleaned by a licensed chimney sweep.

PROBLEMS WITH CHIMNEYS:

This chimney liner has a crack that should be checked by a professional. Such cracks can become very expensive fixes.

This chimney liner is also cracked.

This chimney has a large crack. When you see something like this, you should call a licensed chimney sweep to inspect it.

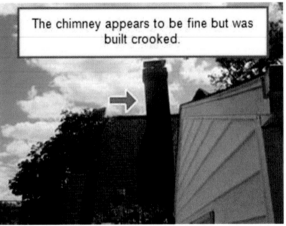

The chimney appears to be fine but was built crooked.

This chimney is very crooked. We called in a licensed chimney sweep to inspect it and found the chimney to be in excellent condition because it was originally built crooked. When you see something like this, call a professional just to make sure everything is fine. Chimneys can be very expensive to repair or rebuild.

CHIMNEY FLASHING:

Having the home's chimney properly flashed is extremely important, because chimney leaks are one of the most prevalent water leak problems found in homes today. Even when you think the flashing is installed perfectly, we recommend checking the attic and the main floor ceiling around the chimney for leaks or stains.

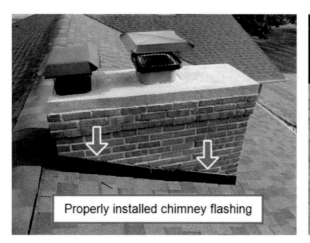

Properly installed chimney flashing

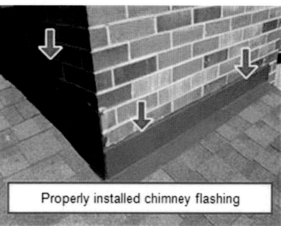

Properly installed chimney flashing

Properly installed chimney flashing

Properly installed chimney cap and flashing

CHIMNEY FLASHING PROBLEMS:

This chimney has been heavily tarred as a poor substitute for being properly flashed.

This chimney has many different issues: probable straight line cracks caused by past chimney fires, poor flashing where the roof and the chimney come together, and a chimney cap on the top of the chimney that needs to be replaced.

This chimney flashing was improperly installed: the flashing is wooden rather than metal. Wood is not recommended as chimney flashing.

This metal step flashing is loose and should be repaired.

CHIMNEY FLASHING PROBLEMS:

Heavily tarring a chimney is a common but improper method of installing flashing.

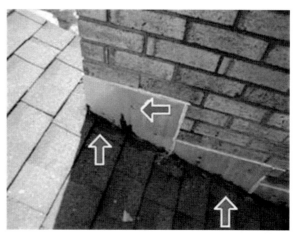

Metal counter flashing was properly installed on this chimney, but the heavily caulked flashing still indicates a possible leak.

This chimney flashing looks great when you are standing on the ground, but when you get close to it you realize that the metal flashing is nothing more than ice and water shield—a material that is intended for use under roof shingles. Yes, it is working, but it will not last long.

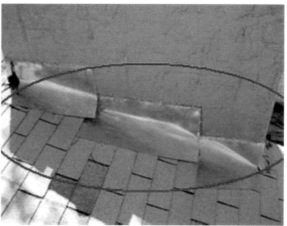

This chimney flashing was not properly installed. We would recommend having this re-flashed by a licensed contractor.

CHIMNEY FLASHING PROBLEMS:

This chimney flashing was installed properly, but the top of the flashing will need to be caulked as part of regular maintenance.

This photo shows where a homeowner has caulked the chimney flashing improperly, using a silicone caulk. We recommend having this caulk removed and new chimney flashings installed.

This chimney has never been properly flashed. Instead, it has been heavily caulked in an effort to prevent water leaks. We recommend having the caulk removed and new chimney flashing installed.

One of the most common problems found on a roof is an improperly flashed chimney.

RUBBER PLUMBING ROOF BOOT FLASHING:

This photo shows a properly installed rubber plumbing exhaust boot on the roof.

A cracked rubber plumbing exhaust boot can cause serious water leaks.

This exhaust pipe has only been caulked and will leak water. We recommend installing a new rubber boot.

This exhaust pipe is too short. We recommend connecting a PVC pipe to it and raising it up by approximately one foot.

Chapter 7
Attic Inspection

Attic ventilation and insulation are extremely important items to inspect. We strongly recommend that this area of the home be looked at very closely, because it is amazing how many homes are not properly ventilated or insulated. One of our inspectors has a home that is approximately ten years old. He watched every aspect of the insulation and ventilation installation during the building process, but after eight years he could not figure out why the snow was melting off the roof so quickly. He went into the attic and found that the blown cellulose in the attic was plugging up the ridge vent and preventing any ridge ventilation. After the ridge vent was replaced, the home's ventilation improved dramatically. The ventilation not only allowed snow to build up on the roof but it also helped in the heating and cooling of the home. As we all know technology is changing rapidly and what worked well ten years ago doesn't always work well today.

MUST-CHECK AREAS:

1. ATTIC ENTRANCE—Entering the attic can be very difficult and you must be careful to clear away as many items and blockages from the entrance as possible, for both your safety and the safety of the current homeowner's possessions. Remember, this is not your house and when you open the attic entrance it is possible that everything from insulation to the homeowner's worldly possessions will fall on you. You are responsible for any mess you make in the house (and any damage), so proceed with caution.

2. ATTIC INSULATION—Based on today's standards, we recommend approximately sixteen inches of insulation inside an attic. Even if you have built a new home and think you have plenty of insulation, you should check the insulation level because it is surprising how many new homes we see that are not insulated properly.

3. ATTIC VENTILATION—Attic ventilation is extremely important, so check that the attic is properly vented. The approximate temperature difference between the home's exterior and the attic should be ten to fifteen degrees Fahrenheit. Poor attic ventilation can cause many problems in the home. If the attic has been improperly ventilated, the heat in the attic can destroy thirty-year shingles in fifteen years or less and can make it difficult for the home to heat and cool properly. It can also cause mold growth, as well as serious ice damage in colder climates.

4. ATTIC VENTILATION AND SOFFIT VENTS—When checking the soffit vents, make sure that the insulation in the house is not covering the soffits. If the soffit vents are covered by insulation or there are not enough soffit vents, air will not flow properly through the attic.

5. ROOF VENTS AND RIDGE VENTS—Roof vents and ridge vents both work well if they are installed properly. Check that the openings are large enough to allow the home to vent. We find that many ridge vents installed today have been cut open only approximately two inches (or one inch on each side of the ridge), but we recommend a 1 ¾ to 2 inch opening on each side of the ridge, for a maximum of four inches, for proper ridge ventilation.

6. MOLD AND MOLD-LIKE SUBSTANCE—Poor ventilation is one reason mold can grow in an attic. If you find mold in the attic we recommend hiring a professional to clean it and install the proper ventilation to prevent the problem from recurring.

7. ROOF SHEATHING AND ROOF BOARDS—When entering the attic, look at the roof sheathing or roof boards. Spotting water leaks and water stains can be difficult, especially if it is not raining or has not rained for several days at the time of the inspection, but you should try to determine if the roof currently leaks or if any water stains are older. Also check around the chimneys—they are common places to find water stains and wood rot.

PROBLEMS WITH ATTIC VENTILATION AND MOLD:

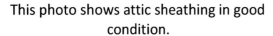

This photo shows attic sheathing in good condition.

There is mold on this attic sheathing. Whenever you think that mold may be present in the attic, call a professional to test it and treat it if necessary. The black and gray areas in the circle in this photo are signs of mold.

This attic sheathing contains mold. Whenever you think that mold may be present, call a professional to test it and treat it if necessary. The black and gray areas in the circle in this photo are signs of mold.

These soffit vents have been blocked by insulation. The blockage will prevent air from venting properly. The soffits are located where the insulation and the roof sheathing boards meet.

ATTICS THAT HAVE RECURRING MOLD PROBLEMS:

All the white in this attic tells you that the attic has been treated for mold. As you look at several of the other photos in this section, keep in mind that if the attic is in good condition the wood will look like normal wood.

The black substance you see in the middle portion of the photo is mold reappearing in the attic after treatment. We recommend calling a professional to remove the mold and to install the proper ventilation and insulation to prevent recurrence of the mold.

The black substance you see on the roof sheathing boards in this attic is a sign of mold reappearing after treatment. The mold may have recurred because the treatment was not performed properly.

PROPER AND IMPROPER INSTALLATION OF ATTIC RIDGE VENTILATION:

This ridge vent has been properly installed. The wood sheathing has been cut open three to 3.5 inches wide.

This ridge vent has never been cut open, so it will not properly vent the home.

A ridge vent should be cut open at least 3.5 inches wide. This one is only one inch wide, so it will not allow proper ventilation of the attic.

This is a photo of a ridge vent plugged with insulation in an attic. We find this problem quite often. A ridge vent that cannot vent properly may cause several other issues in the home.

PROPER INSTALLATION OF ATTIC SOFFIT VENTS:

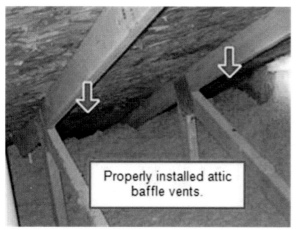

Properly installed attic baffle vents.

Properly installed attic baffle vents.

The arrows in this photo are pointing to the baffles for the soffit vents. The baffles allow the attic to vent properly, while providing additional insulation. We recommend that you check the attic to make sure its soffit vents have the proper ventilation. It is common to find soffit vents in the attic that have been plugged with insulation.

The only difference between these baffles and the ones to the left are that these are made of cardboard, which is a proper material to use.

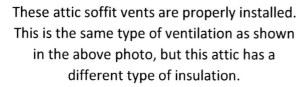

These attic soffit vents are properly installed. This is the same type of ventilation as shown in the above photo, but this attic has a different type of insulation.

These attic soffit vents are also properly installed. This is the same type of ventilation as shown in the above photo, but this attic has a different type of insulation.

TYPES OF ATTIC INSULATION:

Based on today's standards we recommend sixteen to eighteen inches of insulation.

Blown-in fiberglass insulation is commonly found in homes. Its R-value is between 2.20 and 4.30 per inch.

Rolled fiberglass insulation has an R-value between 3.14 and 4.30 per inch.

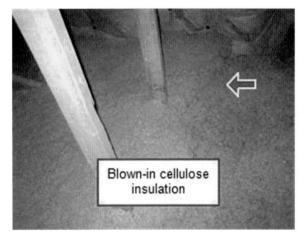

Blown-in attic cellulose insulation. Its R-value is between 3.60 and 3.70 per inch.

Blown-in white fiberglass insulation has an R-value of 2.8 per inch.

ATTICS THAT ARE NOT PROPERLY INSULATED:

This attic has been insulated with approximately 6 inches of blown-in fiberglass. Approximately 8 to 10 inches of additional insulation should be added.

These are blocks of Styrofoam insulation. If you find them in your attic, we recommend replacing them with new insulation of a different type.

Older homes may have only 4 to 6 inches of insulation. More insulation should be added.

PROBLEMS WITH SPLICED ELECTRICAL WIRES IN ATTICS:

When inspecting an attic, try to determine how the bathroom exhaust fans have been wired. Poor wiring jobs are often found in older homes in which the homeowners did the work themselves.

Electrical wires spliced together should be placed in a covered junction box. Junction boxes are intended for safely running electrical wires.

KNOB AND TUBE WIRING:

 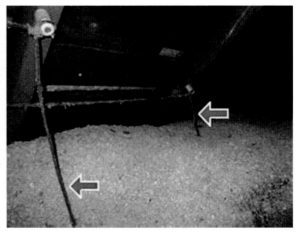

Knob and tube wiring should never have insulation installed around it. If you see knob and tube wiring, contact a licensed contractor. For safety reasons, do not touch the wiring yourself.

PLUMBING WASTE AND BATHROOM FAN VENTS IN THE ATTIC:

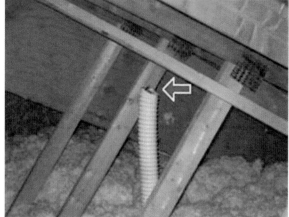

This photo shows a plumbing exhaust vent properly run to the exterior of the home through the roof sheathing.

This bathroom exhaust vent has been run directly into the attic. We recommend that all bathroom shower vents run to the exterior of the home, generally through the soffit vents.

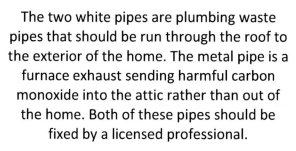

The two white pipes are plumbing waste pipes that should be run through the roof to the exterior of the home. The metal pipe is a furnace exhaust sending harmful carbon monoxide into the attic rather than out of the home. Both of these pipes should be fixed by a licensed professional.

This is a photo of a bathroom vent that was run into the attic instead of to the exterior of the home. All bathroom shower vents should be run to the exterior of the home, generally through the soffit vents. This improperly installed bathroom vent is causing mold to grow on the roof boards.

PROBLEMS WITH THE ATTIC STRUCTURE:

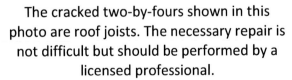

Properly installed knee wall

This photo shows a properly installed knee wall that is providing additional support to the roof structure. The red lines on the left side indicate the knee wall.

When re-supporting roof structures, you cannot install a two-by-four anywhere you wish. Improper installation will cause problems with the home's ceilings. This attic structure was most likely repaired by a homeowner. We recommend hiring a licensed professional to make structural repairs.

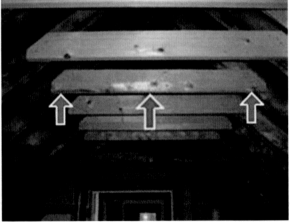

The cracked two-by-fours shown in this photo are roof joists. The necessary repair is not difficult but should be performed by a licensed professional.

Collar ties are used to provide additional support to an attic's roof boards. The boards that are supporting the two sides of the roof together at the top of the photo are collar ties.

PROBLEMS WITH ATTIC AND ROOF SHEATHING:

Properly Installed Roof Sheathing Clips

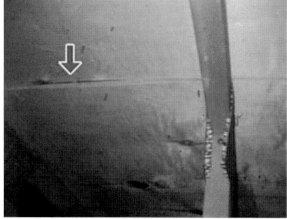

This photo demonstrates what can happen when roof sheathing clips are not installed. The lower section of sheathing has bowed. If a roof sheathing clip had been installed, this would not have happened.

This is a photo of roof sheathing that has no sheathing clips installed and the roof sheathing has dropped.

This is a photo of the lower side of the roof as viewed from the attic. Wooden shake shingles have been placed over the roof boards. This was a normal installation process years ago. The problem with this method is that the roof may have two layers of asphalt shingles on top of this, creating a much greater than acceptable weight load on the roof.

This roof vent was removed, and new shingles were installed over it. The hole should have been re-supported before installing new shingles.

WATER STAINS IN THE ATTIC:

Water stains were found under this chimney. There was a flashing leak around the exterior of the chimney. A chimney's flashing should be checked for leaks and possibly caulked twice each year.

Water stains are often found in attics, because a small amount of water will always enter through a roof vent or a ridge vent.

Again, water stains in the attic are most commonly found around chimneys. A chimney's flashing should be checked for leaks and possibly caulked twice each year.

Chapter 8
Basement or Crawl-Space Structure Inspection

Inspecting the basement or crawl space of a home is often one of the most difficult yet important parts of the inspection. Major problems that will mean costly repairs can be found there. We cannot explain every part of a basement's structure to you, but we have tried to cover the most common issues we find. Several of these should be repaired by a licensed contractor. Don't just hire the person who offers the best price—make sure that the licensed contractor really understands how to properly repair the structure.

MUST-CHECK AREAS:

1. BASEMENT WALLS—Look at all the basement walls, checking for serious cracks, pushing inward or bowing, and water stains.

2. BASEMENT FLOOR CRACKS—These are very common. When concrete is poured it is moist, then when it dries the moisture goes away and cracks can form. Some builders will install expansion joints to try to control where cracks will appear. This system works well but not perfectly. There is no 100 percent flawless way to prevent concrete cracks.

3. MAIN BASEMENT SUPPORT BEAMS—The main support beam in the basement carries the largest load in the home. Many times a flawed support beam is the reason for floor movement in the main floor of the home. Check the support beams to make sure they are straight, free of wood rot, and free of termites, and that no support posts have been removed. The basement structure is a critical part of the home, so look closely at every part of it.

4. BASEMENT FLOOR JOISTS—Check all floor joists for cracks, wood rot, and other damage. Basement floor joists are another critical part of the basement inspection process, and you need to walk through the entire basement or crawl through the entire crawl space looking at each floor joist. Make sure the floor joists have not been notched by the homeowner so that he or she could add other things to the space, that they are not cracked, and that they do not have a wood-destroying insect infestation.

5. RIM JOISTS—Inspect all rim joists for termites. Check extra closely under main floor exterior doors for wood rot and water leaks. We also recommend that each rim joist be entirely insulated in either spray foam insulation or rolled fiberglass batt insulation.

6. WATER STAINS—Look for water stains around the base of each wall. If the basement contains paneling, look for water stains where the paneling and the basement floor meet. Examine anything that water can stain. Look at the base of the supporting post, the base of the staircase, the base of the furnace (particularly if it is old) and any work benches. Also look at storage units that have been installed. How are the homeowners storing their items—in protective plastic, in cardboard boxes, on the floor, or on shelves? These stored items have normally been in the home for a long time and their condition can tell you a lot whether water is leaking into the home. Sometimes you don't have to be an expert to find problems; you just need to take the time to look.

7. SUMP PUMP—If the home has a sump pump, test to ensure it is operating properly.

8. SEWAGE INJECTOR PUMP—If the house has a septic field, there is a good chance that a sewage injector pump will be located in the basement. Test it by running the water only in the basement and listening for the pump to turn on.

9. CRAWL SPACE—If you are inspecting a home that has a crawl space rather than a basement, although we understand crawl spaces are not fun places to enter, it is extremely important that you go into the crawl space to look at the structure, foundation, and plumbing system. While you are crawling under the house, have somebody above turn on all the water so that you can check for water leaks in the main waste lines and water lines.

10. BASEMENT STAIRS AND RAILINGS—If the home has a basement check the stairs for structural integrity and the railings for safety.

11. BASEMENT WINDOWS—If the home has a basement and its windows are normal basement windows rather than daylight windows, you should consider eventually replacing them with glass-block windows, which improve safety and help prevent water from entering the home.

DIFFERENT TYPES OF BASEMENT STRUCTURES:

The steel I beam serves as the main support beam in this basement. Steel beams are still used today but were commonly used in older homes.

This photo shows a newly installed laminated wood beam.

2x6 main support wall.

DIFFERENT TYPES OF BASEMENT STRUCTURES:

This basement has a steel support beam and steel support posts.

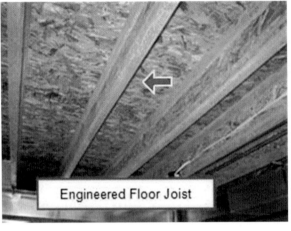

These are engineered floor joists.

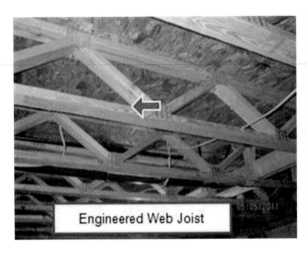

This basement has engineered web floor joists.

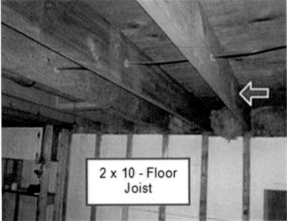

Standard floor joists are two-by-tens.

PROBLEMS WITH BASEMENT STRUCTURES:

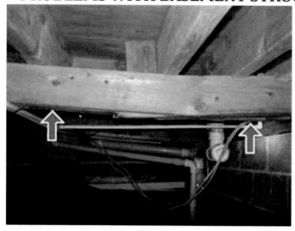

The center of the support beam pictured here has settled due to being undersized. Look closely at the structure to determine if any of beams are damaged or have settled.

The support beam in this basement is over spanned so it's sagging in the middle. It doesn't look bad, but the center of the beam has actually dropped approximately 1½ to 2 inches.

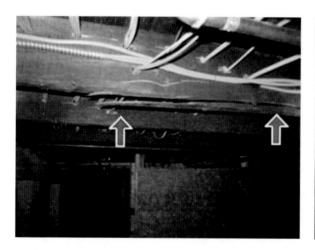

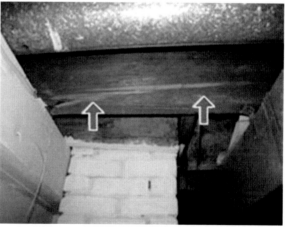

We recommend having any cracked floor joists repaired by a licensed professional. They are generally easy to fix, but the one on the left will be difficult because a lot of wiring is fed through the joist.

PROBLEMS WITH BASEMENT STRUCTURES:

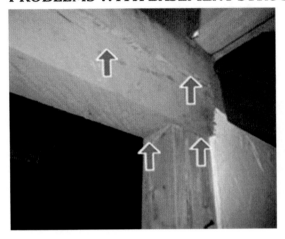

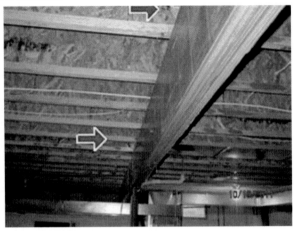

A cracked laminated wood beam requires professional help. The majority of these cracks are perfectly fine, but occasionally they need to be looked at by a licensed professional to make sure they are structurally safe.

Each wood support beam should stand straight up and down, not twisted in either direction. This support beam has shifted approximately one inch and will need to be repaired or replaced.

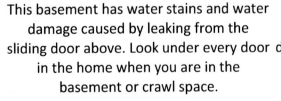

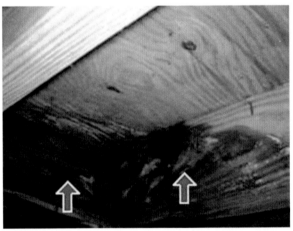

This basement has water stains and water damage caused by leaking from the sliding door above. Look under every door in the home when you are in the basement or crawl space.

Pictured here is a rotted floor joist found underneath the entry door. Look under every door in the home when you are in the basement or crawl space.

PROBLEMS WITH BASEMENT STRUCTURES:

The support post in this basement is carrying too much weight and is bending under the pressure. We recommend hiring a licensed contractor to determine what type of supports should be installed.

This cracked floor joist should be repaired.

The support beam pictured here has twisted by approximately one inch, causing the center of the entire home to drop. Look very closely at each main support beam. They occasionally will lean to one side, but an inch of movement is too much.

The owner of this home has cut into the floor joists, weakening the overall floor structure. The floor joists should all be repaired by a licensed contractor.

PROBLEMS WITH BASEMENT STRUCTURES AND TERMITES:

This basement shows signs of termites. See chapter 17 for more details.

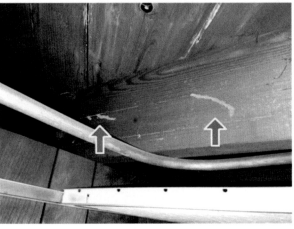

Signs of termites are pictured here. See chapter 17 for more details.

This photo shows a basement with signs of termites. See chapter 17 for more details.

This photo shows how difficult it can be to find termites. The arrow is pointing at one of several small, straight lines of termites that are destroying the interior of this floor joist. If you take a long screw driver, stab it into the wood, and it goes through the board like this one did, you have a problem.

PROBLEMS WITH BASEMENT STRUCTURES:

A car jack should not be used to support a home. We recommend hiring a licensed contractor to install proper supports.

The main beam in this photo is improperly supported by a cinder block with no concrete footing. These types of problems are generally found in older homes.

These two photos are of a brand-new home. The support posts under the basement staircase have bowed by approximately two inches. We recommend having this repaired before moving in.

TYPES OF BASEMENT WALL AND FOUNDATION:

There are three main types of foundation commonly used today in basement and crawl space construction: concrete poured walls, concrete block walls, and concrete slab foundations. Occasionally you will see wooden foundations, and older homes may have stone foundations.

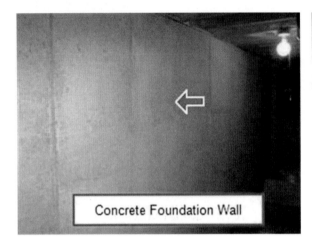

The foundation wall pictured is a concrete poured wall.

This foundation wall is a concrete block wall.

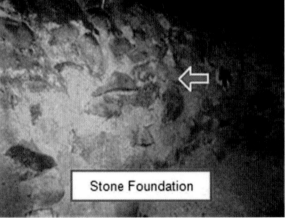

The garage has a precast concrete floor, which is incredibly strong. Precast concrete garage floors are primarily used in industrial settings rather than in homes, but they can be installed on top of a home's basement foundation to allow for an additional storage under the garage.

This is a stone foundation, more likely to be found in an older home than in a newer home.

TYPES OF BASEMENT, SLAB FOUNDATION, AND WALL:

This is a precast foundation wall.

This photo shows a concrete slab foundation that has just been poured.

EVERY BASEMENT WALL SHOULD BE EXAMINED FOR CRACKS AND MOVEMENT

You can view every basement wall by standing in each corner of the basement and looking straight down each wall for any movement such as bowing, bulging, tilting, or sliding of the wall. Most cracks found in basement walls are not of any structural concern, but they may be a concern for leaking.

If water stains or other signs of water are found, the crack should be repaired by a waterproofing and damp-proofing company. If you have found the basement walls are not straight, have a professional check for major structural concerns. Whether finished or unfinished, 90 to 95 percent of basements will experience some kind of water penetration.

PROBLEMS WITH FOUNDATION WALL CRACKS:

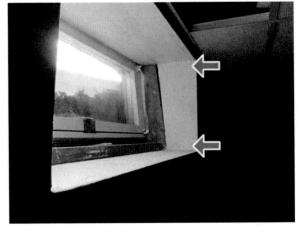

This concrete block basement foundation wall has a crack. The wall should be checked by a professional foundation specialist.

When you are in a basement and all the foundation walls have been covered with drywall, continue looking for anything that looks odd, like this window. After seeing this window we determined that the foundation behind the window moved in approximately 6 inches. This is a major problem and the wall will need serious repairs.

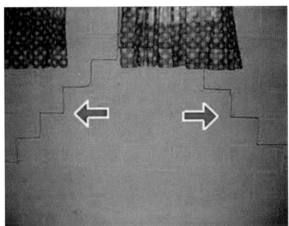

This concrete block basement foundation wall has bowed. We recommend having it checked by a professional foundation specialist.

This photo shows a large step crack in a concrete block basement foundation wall. Again, these cracks are generally not a structural concern. However, if you are concerned, call a professional foundation expert.

FOUNDATION-CRACK AND WATER-LEAK REPAIRS:

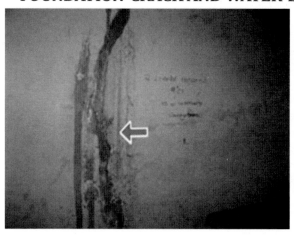
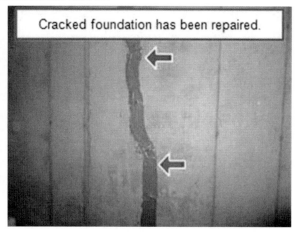

This crack has been repaired by epoxy injection, a method in which a professional company injects epoxy into a foundation crack to stop the basement foundation from leaking.

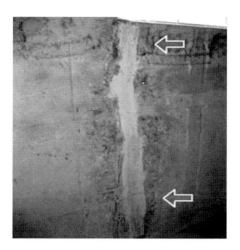
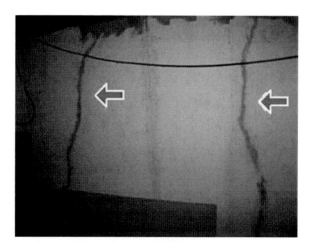

This is a basement wall that has been repaired in response to leaks that occurred in the past.

CRACKED OR BOWED BASEMENT FOUNDATION REPAIRED BY A PROFESSIONAL:

This block wall foundation has been secured with a steel plate wall anchor. We have found this type of repair to be very successful.

Properly installed steel I-beams with no current structural concerns.

The supporting system was installed using steel I beams. This is generally a very successful way of re-supporting a foundation, but in this case the wall has continued to move and is pushing the I-beams inward and the wall will need to be re supported.

BASEMENT AND CRAWL SPACE INSULATION:

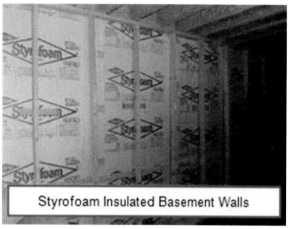

In our opinion, spray foaming the walls and ceiling of a crawl space is the best way to insulate it for energy efficiency.

This basement has Styrofoam insulation on its walls.

This crawl space has reflective insulation.

Fiberglass insulation can also be used on the walls of a crawl space.

BASEMENT AND CRAWLSPACE INSULATION:

In this basement fiberglass wall insulation with paper moisture barrier has been installed.

Spray foam insulation has been installed in the rim box and rim joists in this basement's ceiling. Insulating the rim box is very important since it is considered a prime area for heat loss.

This rim box is not insulated. We recommend that rim boxes around the entire basement or crawl space be insulated.

In this basement we found evidence of a water stain behind the insulation in the rim box. The leak is coming from above or from the exterior of the home. Look behind the insulation in every rim joist and rim box.

BASEMENT WINDOW INSPECTION:

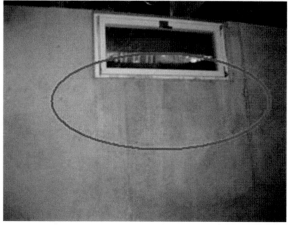

This is a typical glass block window. We recommend replacing all basement windows with glass block windows, which are safer and better at preventing water from entering the home.

Here we see evidence of water leaking from a basement window.

The glass block window in this photo is leaking, because the dirt on the home's exterior was built up above window level.

Old basement windows should be replaced for safety, energy efficiency, and prevention of water leaks.

BASEMENT AND CRAWL SPACE WATER LEAKS AND STAINS:

This basement has current water leaks. Depending on when you look at your new home, it may be very difficult for you or a professional inspector to determine whether the basement currently has a leak.

Basement water stains show up well on wood paneling, making examination of paneling one of the easiest ways to find water stains or current leaks. The paneling absorbs water, and the resulting stains remain on the paneling forever.

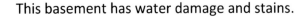

This basement has water damage and stains.

Water can enter the home where the concrete ends and the house framing begins. This is a common place to find leaks, so examine it closely.

BASEMENT AND CRAWL SPACE WATER LEAKS AND STAINS:

When looking for water stains in the basement, look very closely at each wall. Also, take note of what the homeowner has stored on the basement floor and whether the stored items are in plastic containers or in cardboard boxes. These clues may help you to figure out if the basement leaks.

Always look into a crawl space, even if the homeowner has blocked it off. We recommend asking the homeowner to remove any items that are blocking the entry so you can properly view inside.

This crawl space has evidence of a water leak. Dirt crawl spaces should be covered with plastic to help reduce moisture.

BASEMENT DEWATERING SYSTEM INSPECTION:

The gray area around the wall represents a dewatering system that was installed.

This metal baseboard drain is another type of dewatering system.

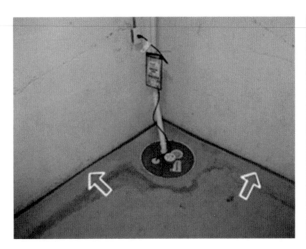

The basement floor concrete was cut, a dewatering system was installed, and then it was refilled with concrete.

This picture shows another type of dewatering system we have found while doing inspections.

We know that several portions of this book have mentioned that sump pumps should be plugged into a GFCI outlet. We recommend talking to your local code inspector; sometimes they allow a single-outlet plug rather than requiring a double-outlet plug. If the power goes out, the GFCI pops, and you do not check the sump pump, the basement could flood if you live in an area that has a high water table.

BASEMENT STAIRS AND RAILINGS:

Check that basement stairs are structurally sound, with no severe movement, and with well-secured treads. For safety any set of basement stairs that has more than three steps should have railings. Make sure all railings are secured to the wall and have very little movement.

Chapter 9
Main Water Supply and Water-Line Inspection

Water lines and waste lines must be inspected can have several types of issues. As inspectors, we cannot determine the interior conditions of the underground waste lines that connect to the city lines. However, we often recommend, primarily for older homes, having the waste lines that run from the home to the main city waste lines checked by a professional with a camera system. We recently requested that this be done for a seventy-five-year-old home surrounded by several trees, and the company found $10,000 in repairs that needed to be done.

MUST-CHECK AREAS

1. PVC AND ABS PLUMBING WASTE LINES—In today's home repair and new home construction, the white pipes are PVC and the black pipes are ABS. These waste lines generally don't have many major issues. The most important thing to do is to flush the toilets, run the water for a few minutes, and look for leaks. When looking for leaks, don't just look up at the plumbing waste lines—look at the floor for small puddles of dripping water, because you can very easily miss slow drips if you just look overhead. It may sound unconventional, but for many aspects of basement inspection, including plumbing, we turn off the lights and use a high-powered flashlight to find problems.

2. CAST-IRON WASTEWATER LINES—Cast-iron wastewater lines have been being used in homes for approximately one-hundred-fifty years, and they may continue to be used for many years to come. Look closely at these pipes, checking for cracks, corrosion, or holes, including on the top side of the pipes. We find many holes on the top side of these lines. Homeowners rarely notice these holes if they are not currently leaking in the home. If you find any of these problems, have the lines replaced.

3. GALVANIZED WASTE LINES—Galvanized waste lines are silver. We find very few problems with these lines. The most serious problem we come across occasionally is corrosion buildup in the interior of the line, which eventually plugs the line. At that point the line must be replaced. Corrosion buildup may exist if you see slow draining when running the water. The only way to proactively check for corrosion buildup is to hire a company to run a camera test through the home's wastewater lines.

4. LEAD WASTE LINES—We find very few problems with lead waste lines. However, because they are soft they can be damaged easily.

4. **COPPER WASTE LINES**—Copper is an excellent material for waste line functionality but very expensive, therefore we find very few copper waste lines in the homes we inspect.

INTERIOR WATER LINES:

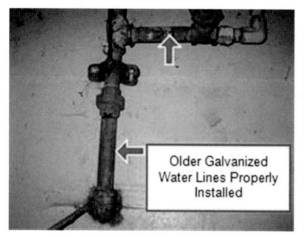

Galvanized water lines are generally found only in older homes. Sometimes they corrode from the interior, plugging up and slowing or stopping water flow through the home.

CPVC water lines properly installed.

PEX water lines are generally red or blue. They are used more today as a less expensive, easy-to-install substitute for copper.

These water lines are made of copper.

MAIN WATER SUPPLY:

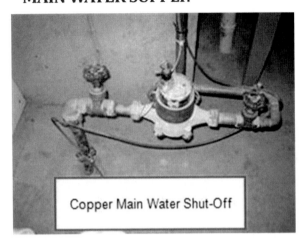

Copper Main Water Shut-Off

This photo shows a copper main water supply. A main water supply is the connection that allows water to flow between the home and the city water supply.

This water supply is made of lead. The "bubble" the arrow is pointing at is the sign that this is a lead water supply. These are found in many older homes. Replacing this with a copper line costs approximately $3,000 to $5,000 or more.

A galvanized main water supply, such as the one shown in this photo, was often used for installation several years ago.

Polybutylene main water supply piping was used extensively from 1978 until 1995. This material is known for its failure issues. You should research this material and talk to a local contractor for advice when these lines are found.

LOOK FOR THE FOLLOWING WHEN INSPECTING WATER LINES:

- Water leaks in all water-line joints.
- Water leaks in all shut-off valves.
- Galvanized and copper pipes should be connected by a dielectric union pipe fitting, which is designed to hold together two different types of metal and prevent corrosion.
- Galvanized lines that run horizontally through the house may build up corrosion which blocks water. Run at least two faucets at the same time, and check that the water pressure is adequate.

INTERIOR WATER LINES:

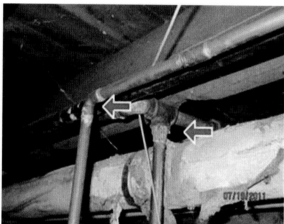

The water heater lines shown in this photo were properly installed using dielectric unions. Dielectric unions are designed to connect different types of metal, such as copper and galvanized pipes.

Remember to look very closely at all the water lines for small leaks and slow drips.

COMMONLY USED WATER HEATERS:

HIGH-EFFICIENCY WATER HEATER: The easiest way to determine if the water heater is a high-efficiency unit is to check if the exhaust vents out the side of the home through PVC plastic pipe.

REGULAR/BASIC WATER HEATER: This type of water heater is vented out a chimney on the roof or up a metal liner through the roof.

TANKLESS WATER HEATER: This is the newest type of water heater. It is much smaller than the other types and is attached to the wall of the home.

ELECTRIC WATER HEATER: Electric water heaters do not need to be vented.

Electric water heater

Gas water heater

Tankless water heater

The white PVC exhaust pipes in this photo indicate that the water heater is a high-efficiency unit.

LOOK FOR THE FOLLOWING WHEN INSPECTING A WATER HEATER:

1. Check that the water heater is producing hot water.

2. The temperature and pressure (T&P) relief valve should have a pipe extended six inches from the floor.

3. The water-heater flue should be properly connected with a minimum of three screws per joint.

4. All water-heater flues run into a chimney should be properly connected to prevent carbon monoxide from entering the home.

5. A gurgling sound coming from the water heater is an indicator that the hot water has sediment buildup at the bottom of the inside of the tank and the water heater is nearing the end of its useful life.

6. Many water heaters are installed by the homeowner and may not be vented properly. We recommend having a local plumbing inspector perform a venting inspection.

7. Check that the draft hood is securely connected to the water heater.

8. Make sure the water-heater flue has positive air flow to the chimney or the roof.

9. If a water heater is installed in a closet and is not a high-efficiency unit, it should have louvered doors as well as a vent (typically metal) coming in from the exterior of the home to provide ambient air.

PROBLEMS WITH ELECTRIC WATER HEATERS:

This electric water heater was wired properly with the electrical wires run in a metal conduit and placed in the water heater electrical box. Either nonflexible metal conduit, like that shown in this photo, or flexible metal conduit, like shown in the photo to the right, can be used.

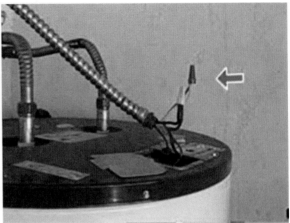

The electrical wires need to be properly secured below the protective steel plate for safety.

PROPERLY EXHAUSTED GAS WATER HEATERS:

This water-heater exhaust line has been properly installed with a new metal liner running from the water heater to the chimney and cement around the water-heater flue for safety and to prevent carbon monoxide from coming back into the home.

The water-heater exhaust shown in this photo has been properly installed. The next set of photos will show several ways a water-heater flue should not be installed.

PROBLEMS WITH WATER-HEATER EXHAUST:

We recommend that the gap around the water-heater exhaust be filled with concrete to prevent carbon monoxide exhaust from entering the home.

The water-heater exhaust above uses dryer-vent material. This type of improper venting is common to water heaters that have been installed by homeowners. This installation poses a safety hazard.

These two water heaters are vented together—an improper installation that poses a safety hazard.

Exhaust should have a positive upward draft, not a downward flow. The exhaust setup in this photo poses a safety hazard and a professional should be called in to repair it.

PROBLEMS WITH WATER-HEATER GAS LINES:

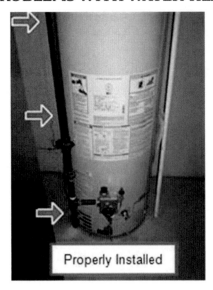

The black-pipe gas line for this water heater has been properly installed.

The gas line black-pipe and flex-pipe for this water heater has been properly installed.

This water heater has been improperly installed. It is connected to a soft, flexible metal line that can be bent, kinked, or broken.

This is another photo of a water heater with an improperly installed gas line. We recommend having a professional contractor make all necessary repairs.

PROBLEMS WITH WATER-HEATER DRIP PIPES:

Properly installed water heater T/P valve drip pipe.

Missing the water heater T/P valve drip pipe.

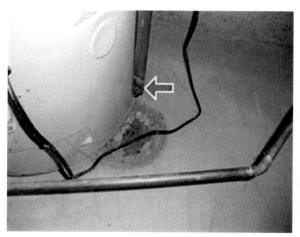

The water heater in this photo is leaking water from its drip pipe. The T/P valve may be going bad—it should be checked by a licensed plumber.

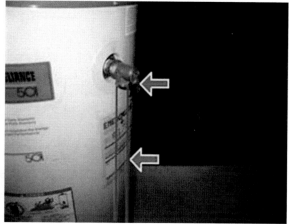

This water heater is missing the drip pipe. For safety, a drip pipe should extend down to six inches above the floor. We recommend using copper or specialized PVC pipe.

WATER-HEATER DRAFT HOOD:

A properly installed draft hood is connected to the water-heater exhaust with three screws per joint.

The exhaust needs three screws per joint to properly fasten it to the water-heater draft hood.

PROBLEMS WITH WATER-HEATER SHUT-OFF VALVES:

This is an older water heater and it is missing the cold-water shut-off valve.

Every water heater should have a main shut-off valve on the cold water side.

PROBLEMS WITH WATER HEATERS:

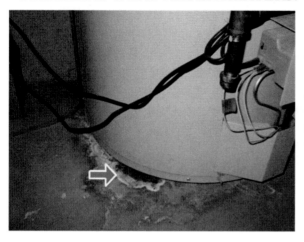

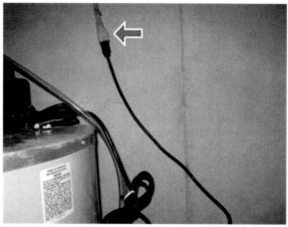

This photo shows rust at the base of the water heater. After looking at the unit closely, we found there was a slow water leak.

A high-efficiency water heater always uses a power (electric) vent. We don't recommend running an extension cord to the water heater, as shown in this photo. We recommend hiring a licensed electrician to install a dedicated outlet.

This water heater shows signs of burning, caused by back-drafting, at its base. We recommend having a licensed HVAC or plumbing contractor check the unit for this safety hazard.

When you have a hot water heater with a metal chimney flu you should never use a flexible aluminum water line. These are for high-efficiency hot water heaters. Install two flexible copper water lines.

PLUMBING WASTE LINE INSPECTION:

PVC—PVC is the most commonly found plumbing waste line material found in new homes today. PVC is white and the size normally used for main waste lines is three to four inches in diameter. PVC is also used for interior waste lines coming from the kitchen and bath. Those lines are normally 2 to 2 ½ inches in diameter, with the exception of toilet lines, which are normally three to four inches. These pipes should have a long, dependable life if not damaged.

GALVANIZED STEEL—Galvanized steel is found mainly in older homes and has a life expectancy of fifty to seventy-five years. We recommend looking closely at the pipes for rust that may cause future problems.

COPPER—Copper is a high-quality material that was used in pipes in the 1950s and 1960s. It was commonly used for drains in bathrooms and kitchens. Sometimes you will also find main waste lines that are copper.

BLACK CAST IRON AND LEAD—These materials are commonly found in older homes. This type of pipe can last between fifty and 100 years or more.

PLUMBING SEPTIC WASTE LINES:

A plumbing waste line that is installed halfway up the basement wall and runs to the exterior of the home generally indicates that the home has a septic system. If you see this in an older home without a septic system, it means that the home has been switched to a city sewage system.

This photo shows an above-ground lift station. This type of unit is generally found only in homes that have been remodeled. Installing this type of unit is much easier than cutting into the concrete and running a new waste line. This system is also used with a septic system.

PROBLEMS WITH PLUMBING WASTE LINES:

THE MOST COMMON PROBLEM AREAS ARE:

- Leaks under toilets.
- Leaks under bathtubs and sinks.
- Severe rusting of cast-iron and galvanized lines (remember, this material is very old).

We recommend that you run all the water in the home for a few minutes. This includes flushing all toilets and checking for leaks under all waste lines in the basement. Also, check for water stains, drywall repairs, or plaster repairs on main-floor ceilings directly under second-story bathrooms.

The cast-iron main waste line pictured here is cracked.

This cast-iron main waste line has cracked and been patched. It should be examined and possibly repaired or replaced by a licensed plumber.

PLUMBING WASTE LINES:

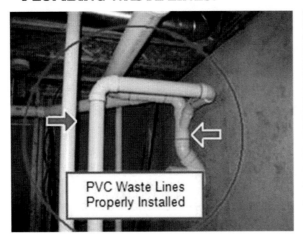

The white pipes shown here are PVC, commonly found in newer homes and used for main waste lines and drains.

Black cast iron waste line was commonly used in older homes and is still used today.

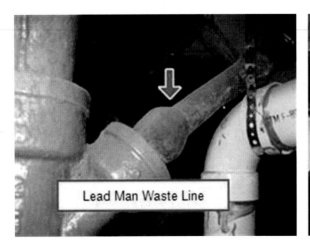

The main waste line in this photo is made of lead.

When inspecting a home that has old cast-iron waste lines, put your hand on the top of the waste line to check for cracks in the line like exist in this photo.

PROBLEMS WITH PLUMBING WASTE LINES:

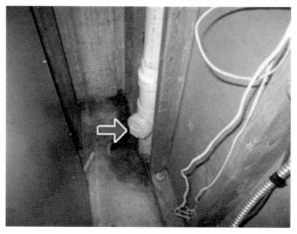

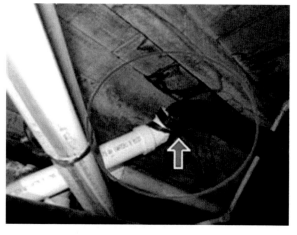

This plumbing line clean out is leaking.

This drain pipe has been improperly installed by taping flexible pipe duct to PVC pipe.

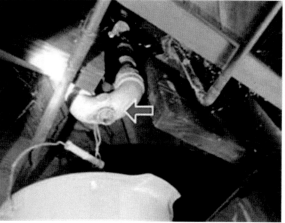

Here we see a water leak under the bathroom toilet. You should flush every toilet in the home, then go below and check for leaks.

This photo shows a water leak under a bathroom tub, as seen from the basement. Leaks under the bathroom tub are common, so you should run water in the bathtub and shower then check for leaks below. Do not walk away from the bathtub or shower while running water, in case there is a leak you are not aware of in that area.

SEWAGE INJECTOR INSPECTION:

A sewage injector pump is a lift station for bathroom waste. Each of these pumps should have two waste lines coming out of it. One line is for waste and the other line runs to the exterior of the home for venting.

The pump can be tested by flushing the toilet or running water for a couple minutes. When you hear the pump engage you will know it is operating.

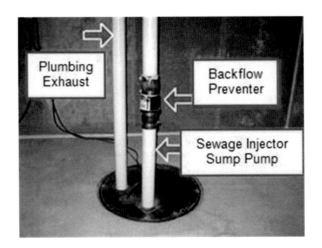

The sewage injector cover needs to be sealed around the pipes to prevent sewage gas from escaping.

A sewage injector is used for many purposes in a home but most commonly used for lifting bathroom wastewater and laundry wastewater, also known as gray water, up to your plumbing system.

SUMP PUMPS AND BACK-UP SUMP PUMP SYSTEMS:

Properly Installed

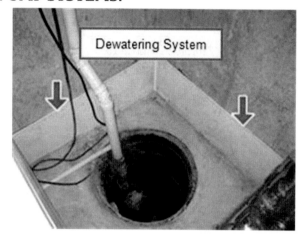

Dewatering System

This sump pump has been properly installed with a backflow preventer (the red arrow is pointing at it). We recommend that all sump pumps have backflow preventers.

This sump pump was installed with a dewatering system for the basement. A dewatering system, when properly installed, will divert water to the sump pump, preventing it from entering the basement. The water will be lifted out and away from the home.

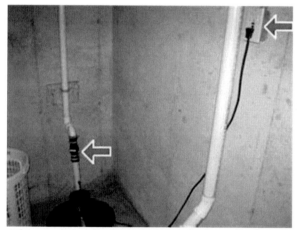

This sump pump was properly installed and wired to a GFCI outlet, but always remember if the GFCI outlet were to trip then your sump pump would no longer operate until you reset the outlet. This is why you should install some type of backup system or even an alarm to protect your home from flooding in the basement.

This is a photo of a Sump Jet, a sump pump backup system. The Sump Jet will take over as your sump pump and will continue running when there is a power outage at your home. The Sump Jet system is built in just above your sump pump. In our opinion, these are great systems and very reliable.

SUMP PUMP PLUGS:

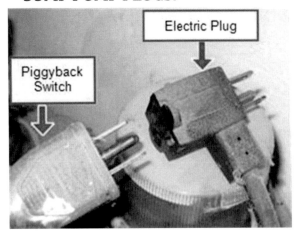

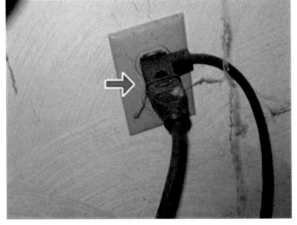

This type of sump pump plug allows you to remove the two plugs from the wall, remove the piggyback switch from the electrical plug, and plug the piggyback switch into the wall to test the sump pump.

This photo shows a plugged-in sump pump sewer injector plug with piggyback switch.

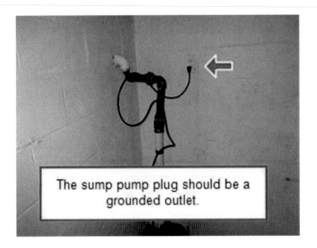

The sump pump plug should be a grounded outlet.

All sump pumps should be wired to a grounded GFCI outlet.

Chapter 10
Heating and Cooling Inspection

Heating and cooling systems are difficult to inspect because the necessary test equipment is very expensive. Our recommendation is that you do a basic check of the system by turning it on and running it for a few minutes, or you simply hire a professional contractor to perform the inspection. We will still provide an overview of some problem areas you can look for as a homeowner.

MUST-CHECK AREAS:

1. TURNING ON THE HEATING SYSTEM—Turn on the heating system by using the thermostat, which is generally located on the main floor of the home. If the home has been foreclosed, you would be smart to bring a couple different types of batteries in case the thermostat batteries need to be replaced.

2. FORCED AIR HEATING—If the home has a forced-air heating system, you should check for heat flow in every register in the home. Heat ducts can be dismantled or unplugged. If the house has a finished basement, look for heat ducts there. If the homeowners have finished the basement themselves, they may have improperly installed the heat ducts.

3. FURNACE FLUE—If the furnace has a metal exhaust, check it for rusting holes but be careful because the metal can get very hot. If the house has a high-efficiency furnace, for safety reasons the exhaust should be made entirely of double-walled PVC liner.

4. HEATING ELECTRICAL—No matter what type of furnace, it must be wired directly to the main panel on a completely separate circuit. Follow this wire back to the main panel and make sure that it is not spliced or connected to anything else.

5. COLD-AIR RETURNS—The major problem we find with cold-air returns is that homeowners who finish their basements on their own may not install the proper cold-air returns.

6. BOILER HEATING—If the home has a boiler heating system, turn on the system and check that all heat registers have heat coming out of them.

7. RADIANT IN-FLOOR HEATING—If the home has radiant in-floor heating, check it by turning on the system. After ten to fifteen minutes, you should be able to feel the heat feeding into the water lines in the floor.

8. GEOTHERMAL HEATING SYSTEM—We recommend always hiring a professional HVAC contractor to check a geothermal heating system whether you or a professional home inspector is performing the home inspection.

BASIC STEPS FOR INSPECTING A FORCED-AIR FURNACE:

1. Turn off the furnace using the thermostat, generally located on the main floor of the home, or the safety switch located on the outside of the furnace.

2. After the furnace has turned off, check the burners for signs of scorching, rust, dirt, drywall dust, and corrosion.

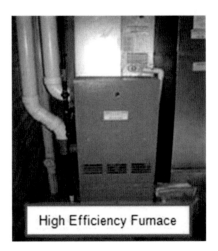

High Efficiency Furnace

3. Turn the unit back on. Stand at least five feet back and off to the side of the furnace to watch for any problems during the ignition process. Problems can include a long-lasting ticking sound, a roaring noise, smoking, flame rollout, or vibration.

4. The heat exchanger is by far the most critical area of the furnace. It is located above the combustion chambers and the burners. Check the heat exchanger for heavy rust or cracks, either of which could cause serious health and safety issues (even death!) in your home.

5. Remove the lower access panel to view the blower. Press and hold the safety switch in to run the blower. Listen for any rattling or squeaking sound coming from the blower. Release the safety switch and inspect the blower for dirt. If the blower is very dirty, we recommend having it cleaned.

80% - 85% Gas Furnace

6. Inspect the flue pipe, checking for rust holes. If you see a small rust hole, tap it lightly with a screwdriver to see if it is rusted all the way through. If the furnace is not a high-efficiency unit, make sure the flue has positive air flow leading to the chimney liner. The chimney liner is normally made of clay or metal.

7. Check that the cold-air returns are connected to the side of the furnace and are found in almost every room of the home.

8. Heat runs should be found in almost every room of the home. However, it is common in some older homes that they were not installed in small bathrooms. Most basements finished by a non-professional will not have proper heat runs or cold-air returns; this lack will cause improper climate control in the basement.

9. Furnace filters are generally located between the furnace and the return air (air flow from the return air to the furnace). Dirty furnace filters will cause the furnace to run less efficiently, increasing energy usage and potentially damaging the furnace. Filters should be cleaned or replaced, depending on the home, every second month.

With the exception of a dirty furnace filter (which may have just been neglected by the homeowner), if you find any issue while completing the above inspection steps, call a licensed HVAC contractor.

PROBLEMS WITH HEATING SYSTEMS:

We never recommend installing a furnace directly on the dirt floor of a crawl space. It should instead be lifted off the ground.

This photo shows rust from moisture leaking in the exhaust, a common problem. If you find such a leak, call a licensed professional to repair it.

This filthy furnace is covered in drywall dust, which may cause problems with operation of the furnace. The furnace should be cleaned.

This is an old gravity-air furnace. Some of these furnaces just don't want to go bad. The problem with these units is that they are very inefficient and costly to remove when having a new furnace installed because they contain asbestos.

PROBLEMS WITH FURNACE EXHAUST:

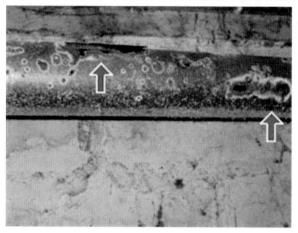

This furnace exhaust contains holes so is not safe.

The exhaust line shown here contains a hole, which is allowing harmful carbon monoxide to enter into the home.

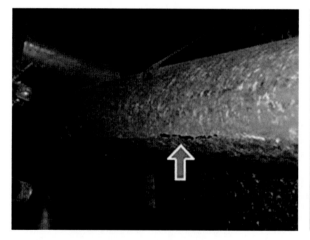

This exhaust line also contains a hole.

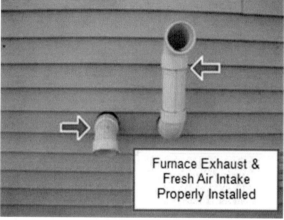

This furnace exhaust has been properly installed.

PROBLEMS WITH HIGH-EFFICIENCY FURNACE EXHAUST:

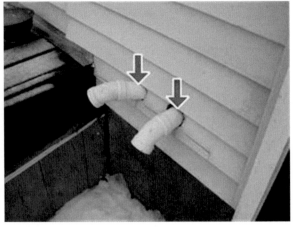

This furnace exhaust is missing an elbow.

This furnace exhaust has not been properly installed. As the furnace exhausts, it sucks the exhaust back into the home through the fresh-air intake. The improper installation poses a safety hazard.

PROBLEMS WITH COLD-AIR RETURNS:

This forced-air furnace has a properly installed cold-air return.

This cold-air return has no cover. We recommend having a cover installed.

PROBLEMS WITH FURNACE WIRING:

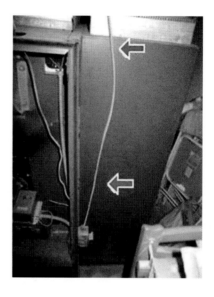

Properly installed electrical wire feeds this furnace.

This furnace wire is not properly installed. Electrical wire not contained by a metal conduit poses a safety hazard.

MISCELLANEOUS FURNACE PROBLEMS:

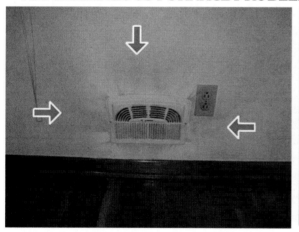

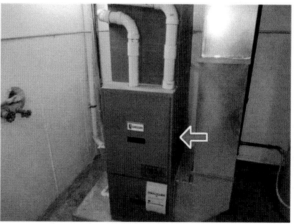

When you see black smoke stains around a home's registers, the furnace probably has a cracked heat changer. Have a licensed contractor check the heat exchanger for cracks.

Turn every furnace at least five to ten degrees Fahrenheit above the setting currently in use. If the furnace does not run until it reaches the setting level but instead keeps turning on and off, the furnace may be short cycling. Short cycling should be repaired by a licensed contractor.

FURNACE FRESH-AIR INTAKE:

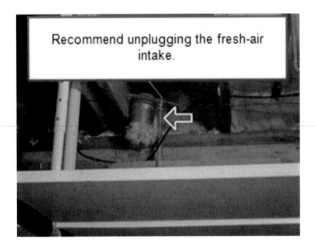

We recommend making sure all the fresh-air intakes found in newer homes are kept unplugged. Many homeowners cover the fresh-air intakes with insulation when they feel cold air coming back into their home because they think it is costing them money. Fresh-air intake is very important for the operation of furnaces, though, so keep the intakes unplugged.

FURNACE GAS LINES:

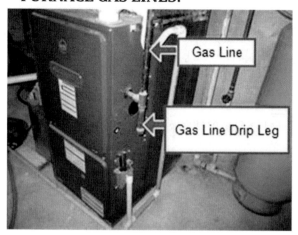

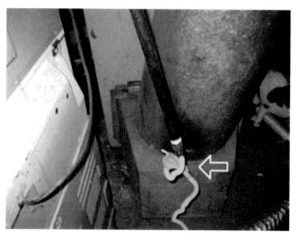

This furnace gas line has been properly installed.

This furnace gas line is not properly installed.

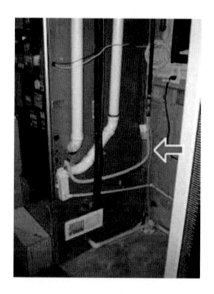

The gas line that has been used for this furnace is intended for appliances only. Read the information on the furnace gas line if it is available—this one clearly states that it is for appliances.

The sediment trap and drip leg is missing from this furnace. This collects gas sediment so it does not enter the furnace.

FURNACE FILTERS:

Electronic Air Cleaner

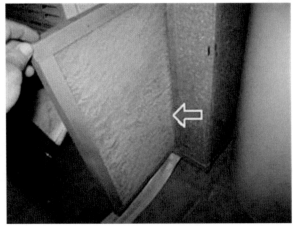

This is a photo of an electronic air cleaner. When they operate, they're great. As home inspectors, we find more of these not operating than operating. Push the test button on the cleaner while the furnace is operating, and listen for a snapping sound that indicates the unit is operating. The inside of these units must be kept clean; if it is not clean, we recommend having a HVAC contractor clean it.

This is a photo of a furnace air filter. There are several types of filters on the market today. We don't recommend any specific one; we only recommend that you replace them with new, clean filters as needed. Approximately 25 percent of furnaces we see while doing home inspections have dirty furnace filters. Dirty filters reduce the efficiency of the furnace by making it work harder than it should. At the worst, the furnace may shut off and you will end up calling a HVAC contractor.

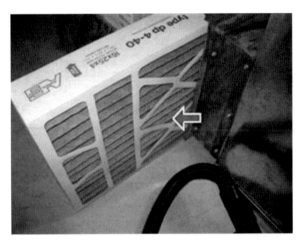

Even if you have one of these larger filters that supposedly should only need to be changed once a year, if you have dirty air ducts you may need to change the filter every six months.

HUMIDIFIERS AND THERMOSTATS:

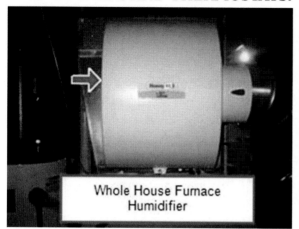

Whole House Furnace Humidifier

Programmable Thermostat Properly Installed

A flow-through furnace humidifier is the most common type found in homes today.

We recommend that all homes have a programmable thermostat installed for energy savings.

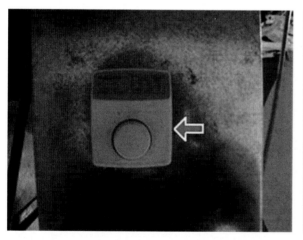

The furnace humidifier thermostat is normally located on the furnace or next to the furnace thermostat on the main floor of the home.

This flow-through humidifier filter is dirty. Humidifier filters should be inspected monthly during winter and cleaned if they are dirty.

HUMIDIFIERS AND THERMOSTATS:

If the furnace has a drum-unit humidifier, we recommend that you be extra-diligent in keeping the unit clean.

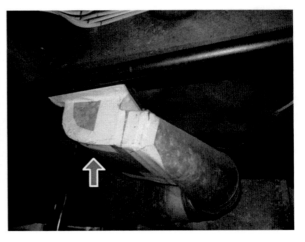

The white wrap on this heating duct is most likely asbestos, which was commonly used years ago. We recommend having all asbestos removed or sealed up by a professional.

This photo shows a condensate pump, which removes condensation from the furnace and air-conditioning unit.

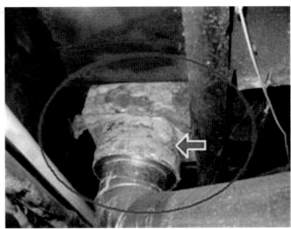

This heating duct has evidence of asbestos. We recommend having all asbestos removed or sealed up by a professional.

ASBESTOS BOILER-LINE PROBLEMS:

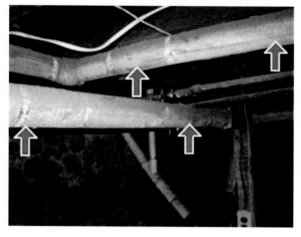
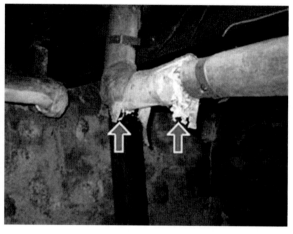

This is a photo of asbestos insulation wrapped around the water lines for a boiler heating system.

This asbestos is in very poor condition. It is what you call friable (easily crumbled or pulverized) asbestos. This poses a serious safety hazard. We recommend having all asbestos removed or sealed up by a professional.

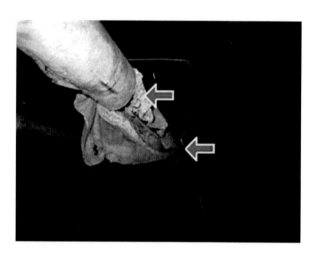

This is another photo of asbestos in very poor condition. Again, friable asbestos, which poses a serious safety hazard. We recommend having all asbestos removed or sealed up by a professional.

AIR CONDITIONING UNIT INSPECTION

1. We recommend that the air conditioning (AC) be turned on to be tested only if the exterior temperature is above sixty-five degrees Fahrenheit. If temperatures are not above sixty-five degrees, you risk damaging the unit. If the home is located in a cold climate, the AC cannot be tested during the winter.

2. External temperature permitting, run the AC to make sure it cools the home properly.

3. Check the line set for signs of freezing. The line set is the line that runs from the AC coil above the furnace to the condenser on the home's exterior.

4. Make sure the compressor is running smoothly and not vibrating. Make sure it is clean, clear of all vegetation, and sitting level.

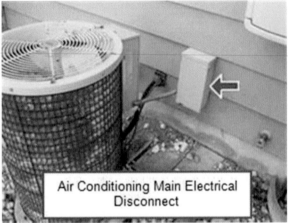

Air Conditioning Main Electrical Disconnect

We recommend that the AC unit sit level.   All air conditioning systems should have a main electrical shut-off on the exterior of the home near the compressor.

PROBLEMS WITH AIR CONDITIONING SYSTEMS:

This is an example of a dirty AC unit. It is important to keep the AC unit clean, but use caution when cleaning it. You don't want to damage the fins. We recommend calling a HVAC contractor to properly clean the unit.

The fins of this AC unit have been damaged, which generally happens when a homeowner cleans the unit.

Vegetation must be kept clear of the AC unit.

PROBLEMS WITH AIR CONDITIONING SYSTEMS:

We recommend that the AC line be wrapped in foam insulation.

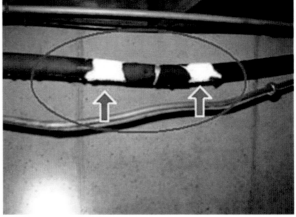

A frozen line set inhibits the flow of coolant and reduces the efficiency of the AC unit. This frozen line set was found in a basement.

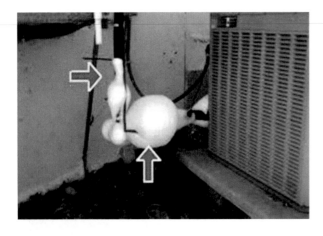

This is another example of ice buildup on the line set connected to the condenser. We recommend having a licensed contractor make all necessary repairs.

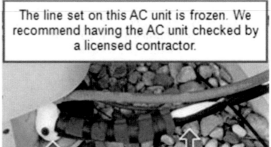

The line set on this AC unit is frozen. We recommend having the AC unit checked by a licensed contractor.

There is ice buildup on this line set connected to the condenser. We recommend having a licensed HVAC contractor make all necessary repairs.

Chapter 11
Electrical Inspection

When inspecting a home, if you are not 100 percent comfortable with removing a main electrical panel we recommend you hire a professional home inspector or a licensed electrician to check the panel for you. We cannot provide you with all the information needed to find a flawed electrical panel, but we will give you an overview of a few common mistakes that homeowners make when installing electrical equipment themselves.

MUST-CHECK AREAS

1. FINDING THE MAIN ELECTRICAL PANEL—Finding the main panel is sometimes difficult. If the home has a basement the electrical panel is generally located there, but if the home does not have a basement or crawl space, the electrical panel is generally located on an exterior wall or inside the garage. The panel will typically be near the main electrical box. You may have to look very closely, because homeowners often cover up these panels with paintings or other household goods.

2. MAIN ELECTRICAL PANEL SAFETY HAZARD—There should always be a three-foot clearance around the electrical panel for safety. Water lines or waste plumbing lines should not be present directly above the electrical panel.

3. MAIN ELECTRICAL PANEL—When checking the main electrical panel, the first thing you should do is to very carefully remove the panel cover. Then look at the three main wires feeding into the panel, and make sure these wires are properly installed and are the adequate size for the panel. Second, make sure there is no double tapping off these three main wires. Third, check that all the electrical breakers in the panel size up to the wires that are feeding them and that the panel is properly grounded. Finally, check that none of the breakers have been double tapped. These steps, while relatively basic, cover some of the major problems that we find in a main electrical panel.

4. MAIN ELECTRICAL PANEL SIZE—Most 60-amp services are too small for today's appliances, so we recommend upgrading to at least a 100-amp panel.

    A. We recommend that all main panels have a main disconnect.
    B. If the meter on the outside of the home is round, it has a 60-amp service. If the inside of the home has a new, 100-amp panel, we recommend having a licensed contractor replace the meter base with a new 100-amp meter so that they will match. This mismatch is a very common issue.
    C. Many older homes have smaller main electrical panels. Because of this, when installing central air conditioning, a main disconnect switch is added to the

outside of the panel. This practice is not acceptable in general, but the majority of the time it will be double tapped into the main lugs. This double tapping poses a safety hazard.

    D. No breakers in the main panel should be double tapped. We recommend that a two-pull breaker be installed instead.

5. FEDERAL PACIFIC ELECTRICAL PANELS—These are legal, however there is a possibility that the circuit breakers in them may not trip when shorted, which is an electrical hazard. Licensed electricians' opinions about this panel vary. We recommend you consult a licensed electrician for an analysis and potential correction.

6. KNOB AND TUBE WIRING—Knob and tube wiring was commonly used in the United States from about 1880 to the 1940s. The danger from this wiring comes from its age, improper modifications, and situations in which insulation wraps around the wires. While knob and tube wiring is considered old and is no longer being installed, we have found no code that requires it to be completely removed. Knob and tube is regulated differently in different areas of the country. Some areas require that it be  removed from all accessible locations, while other areas just require that it not to be used in new construction. In fact, it is not permitted in any new home construction today. If you find knob and tube wiring in a home we recommend you hire a licensed contractor to perform a complete safety evaluation of the home, including the attic.

MAIN ELECTRICAL SERVICE:

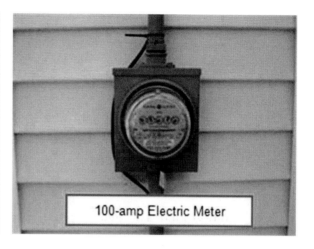

60-amp electrical service generally has a round meter base.

100-amp electrical service generally has a square meter base.

200-amp electrical service is generally shaped like a rectangle.

Double tapping off the main electrical feed wires, a common problem, poses a safety hazard. We recommend that any of the issues below, if present in the home, be repaired by a licensed electrical contractor.

PROBLEMS WITH THE MAIN ELECTRICAL PANEL:

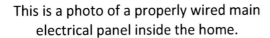

Properly Installed

This is a photo of a properly wired main electrical panel inside the home.

There should be only one wire leading from the main lug that supplies all of the power to the home to each lug. This electrical panel has three wires leading to each lug; the setup poses a safety hazard.

This photo shows double tapping off the main lug. This setup poses a safety hazard. A two-pull breaker should be installed instead.

There should be only one wire leading from the main lug that supplies all power to the home to each lug. This electrical panel has two wires leading to each lug.

PROBLEMS WITH THE MAIN ELECTRICAL PANEL:

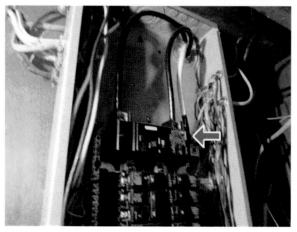 

This 200 amp main electrical panel is mismatched with a 60 amp meter base on the exterior of the home. This would indicate that the main electrical panel was installed by a homeowner or a non-professional. If this were to be installed properly by a licensed contractor and had a city electrical permit the meter base on the exterior of the home would be a rectangle, which would represent a 200 amp electrical service. This electrical service on the exterior the home should be replaced and the entire service be brought up to local standards by a licensed professional.

For safety an electrical panel should have a minimum of three feet of clearance around it.

This is an example of a double-tapped electrical circuit breaker. Only one wire should be feeding into each breaker. We recommend having a licensed electrician make all necessary repairs.

PROBLEMS WITH THE MAIN ELECTRICAL PANEL:

This electrical panel has been properly installed. The arrows show that one wire feeds into each breaker.

The breakers on the top left corner of this panel have rust stains from water entering the panel. The water poses a safety hazard—call an electrician immediately.

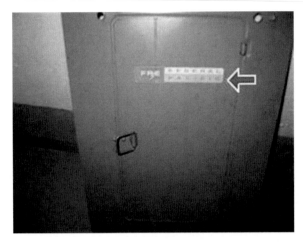

If the home has a Federal Pacific Main Electrical Panel, we recommend having it upgraded to a new panel. The electrical breakers in this panel have been proven not to trip properly when overloaded. This poses a safety hazard.

This is an old electrical fuse panel. We recommend that it be upgraded by a licensed contractor.

PROBLEMS WITH THE MAIN ELECTRICAL PANEL:

Current water leak in the main electric panel, should be repaired by a licensed contractor.

This is a photo of a water pan to protect the electrical panel in the event of a sink plumbing line leak in the main floor bathroom. In this case the local code inspector informed us that it was not a good idea to place a water or waste line directly above an electrical panel, but it was not a code issue. It is difficult to believe this setup would be acceptable anywhere. If you are not sure of an answer, always call a professional.

This electrical panel has a current water leak dropping directly on one of the breakers inside the panel. The water leak is coming from the exterior main electrical supply and should be checked by a licensed electrician.

This is a photo of GFCI breakers inside the main electrical panel. These breakers connect to kitchens, bathrooms, exteriors, garages, or any other area of the home that requires a GFCI outlet.

INTERIOR GROUNDING OF THE MAIN ELECTRICAL PANEL:

Properly Installed

Properly Grounded

This ground wire, hooked up to a water line, has been properly installed.

The main water supply pictured here has a properly installed ground wire connected to its bottom left side.

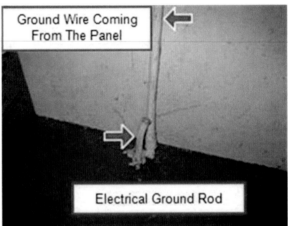

Ground Wire Coming From The Panel

Electrical Ground Rod

The ground wire that is supposed to be attached to this water line is missing. Always check to see if a different ground wire was installed.

This is a photo of an electrical ground rod located directly below the electrical panel in the interior of the home below the basement floor.

ELECTRICAL LIGHT FIXTURES AND PLUGS:

This properly Installed light fixture is wired and connected to a junction box.

Check that light fixtures are properly wired and connected to a junction box.

This photo shows an electrical outlet tester being used. It is an important and inexpensive tool needed for testing outlets in a home.

Properly installed electrical outlet is grounded and has a face plate.

ELECTRICAL OUTLETS AND SWITCHES:

Two-Prong Ungrounded Outlet

GFCI Electrical Outlet - Ground Fault Circuit Interrupter

This photo shows an ungrounded electrical outlet. These are commonly found in older homes.

GFCI outlets are very important, and all exterior, garage, bathroom, and kitchen outlets within six feet of water should be GFCI-protected. When buying or selling a home you should ask the city about local standards.

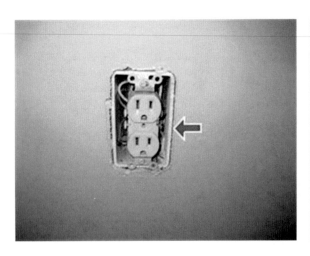

Exterior Outlet

This outlet is missing its electrical face plate. Adding a face plate is a very inexpensive fix for this safety hazard.

This is a photo of an exterior outlet that does not have a GFCI outlet with a reset button. That does NOT mean it is not GFCI-protected, as it may be connected to a GFCI outlet. You should always check these outlets with an electrical outlet tester. Remember, if you trip an outlet, use the reset button to reset it afterward. You don't want to surprise the homeowner with an outlet that needs to be reset.

REVERSE POLARITY:

Reverse polarity occurs when the positive (black) wire has been hooked up to the negative side of the outlet and the negative (white) wire has been hooked up to the positive side outlet. This is not a safety concern, and it is easily fixed by switching the wires.

UNGROUNDED OUTLETS:

Ungrounded outlets are generally found in older homes. Older homes were wired with a two-wire system that did not include a ground wire. Newer wiring includes ground wires. Most homeowners who install their own outlets will typically install a three-prong outlet regardless of whether the outlet is grounded. The correct approach is to only install a two-prong outlet if it is ungrounded or have an electrician install a proper grounded outlet.

SPLICED ELECTRICAL WIRES:

Spliced wires are generally found in areas such as basements, garages, attics, and above ceiling tiles near basement lights. Again, spliced wires are typically found where homeowners have done the work themselves. Look for a wire that has been cut in half and reconnected to another wire, sometimes using just wire nuts. Spliced wires pose a safety hazard, but they should be placed into a junction box.

SPLICED ELECTRICAL WIRES AND JUNCTION BOXES:

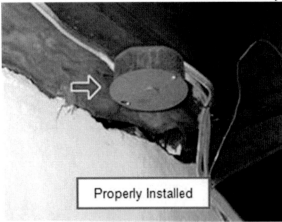

This junction box has been properly installed with a cover.

For safety, spliced electrical wires should always go into a junction box.

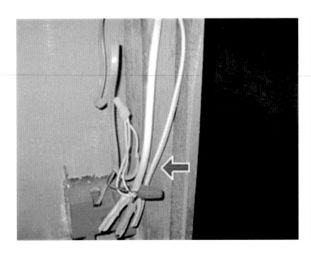

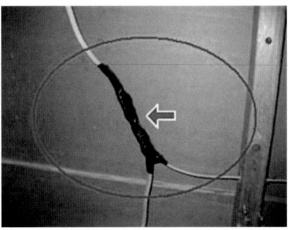

This photo shows another example of spliced wires that do go into a junction box. The lack of junction box poses a safety hazard.

Spliced electrical wires must be placed into the proper junction box for safety.

MISSING JUNCTION BOX COVERS AND FACE PLATES:

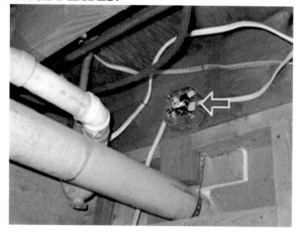

This junction box has been properly installed with a cover.

This electrical junction box is missing its cover. The lack of cover poses a safety hazard.

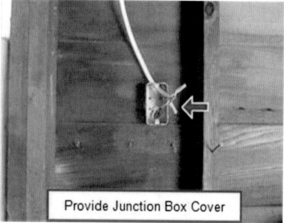

Both of these electrical junction boxes are missing the cover. The lack of a cover poses a safety hazard.

SMOKE DETECTORS:

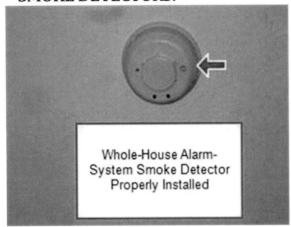

Whole-House Alarm-
System Smoke Detector
Properly Installed

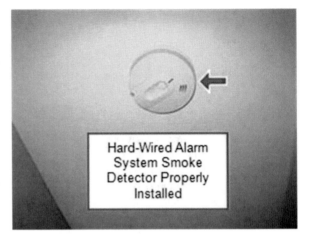

Hard-Wired Alarm
System Smoke
Detector Properly
Installed

This type of smoke detector is found in homes with alarm systems that are hard-wired throughout the home.

This type of smoke detector is hard-wired throughout the home and has a battery backup. To test it, push the test button and hold it down until you hear all the alarms in the home go off. This testing takes only a few seconds.

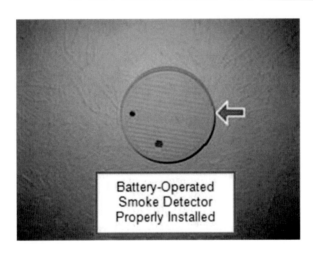

Battery-Operated
Smoke Detector
Properly Installed

This photo shows a simple, battery-operated smoke detector.

Smoke detectors are very important, yet many homes don't contain operational smoke detectors. We recommend having a smoke detector installed in each room, including the basement. When moving into a home, you should replace the batteries in all smoke detectors with new batteries and test the smoke detectors.

We recommend that all smoke detectors more than ten years old be replaced.

Chapter 12
Kitchen Inspection

Several areas need to be checked to determine if there are any major problems in the kitchen.

MUST-CHECK AREAS

1. FLOORS—Look for any cracks in the kitchen tile or damage to any other type of kitchen flooring.

2. COUNTERTOPS—Countertops are generally not problematic, but it is best to look underneath everything because often you will find holes or burn marks that the homeowner has hidden.

3. KITCHEN OUTLETS—We recommend, based on today's standards for safety, that all kitchen outlets be GFCI outlets.

4. GAS OR ELECTRIC—Check if the home is set up for a gas stove, an electric stove, or both.

5. KITCHEN STOVE VENT—If the home has a kitchen stove hood vent, make sure it is set up to vent directly to the home's exterior.

6. OVER-THE-RANGE MICROWAVE—Current minimum standards specify that the microwave should be installed thirteen to sixteen inches above the range. In older homes the microwave was commonly installed less than 13 inches above the range.

7. KITCHEN FAUCET AND UNDER-THE-SINK PLUMBING—Turn on the water in every kitchen faucet and faucet sprayer. Look for water leaks around the faucet, make sure the hot water is operating, and make sure that there is plenty of water pressure. While the water is running, turn on the garbage disposal (if the home has one), and then look below the sink to make sure the plumbing waste lines and water lines are not leaking. Also check below the sink for any water shut-off valves for the hot and cold lines to the faucet and for a shut-off valve for the dishwasher. Sometimes the dishwasher line shut-off can be found in the basement, directly below it, near the ceiling.

8. APPLIANCES—Many home inspection companies say they check appliances, but you should remember that they are doing only a very basic check—just turning the appliances on and off. They will not check the stove's cleaning operation or the dishwasher's various cycles because that would take hours. If you want your appliances thoroughly checked, we recommend calling a professional.

NON-GFCI OUTLETS IN WATER-SOURCE AREAS ARE A SAFETY HAZARD.

GFCI Kitchen Outlet
Properly Installed

GFCI outlets should be located within six feet of the kitchen sink and wet-bar sinks. All outlets in bathrooms, in garages, in unfinished basements and crawl spaces, outdoors, near a pool, or in any other area that may contain moisture should also be GFCI outlets.

This photo shows a non-GFCI outlet in a kitchen, but the outlet is actually connected to a GFCI outlet just to its left. The only way to check these properly is to use an electrical outlet tester.

KITCHEN FAUCETS, SPRAYERS, AND SHUT-OFF VALVES:

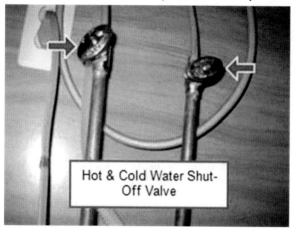

Hot & Cold Water Shut-Off Valve

Dishwasher Water Shut-Off Valve

Check for leaks in the valve under the sink. The kitchen sink faucets should have shut-off valves.

We recommend that all dishwashers have a shut-off valve located under the kitchen sink. You will sometimes find the shut-off valve for the dishwasher in the basement directly below the kitchen.

Check for leaks around each kitchen faucet.

This is a photo of a less expensive kitchen faucet sprayer leaking under the sink. Often you will find a sprayer that is not functioning.

KITCHEN FAUCETS, SPRAYERS AND SHUT-OFF VALVES:

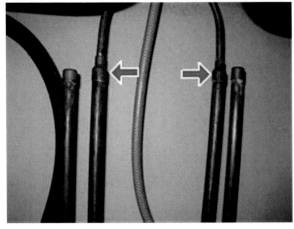

Kitchen faucets and sprayers are common sources of leaks. Although newer and more expensive, this one is leaking.

We recommend that all water lines, hot and cold, and dishwashers have shut-off valves installed.

KITCHEN DRAINS AND PROBLEM AREAS:

Properly Installed

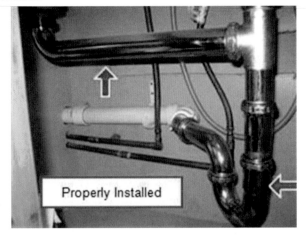

Properly Installed

The plumbing under this kitchen sink has been properly installed.

This plumbing line under the kitchen sink has been run in a metal pipe, which is found generally in higher-end homes.

PROBLEMS WITH KITCHEN DRAINS:

Improper drain installation using electrical tape. We recommend that you look very closely at the plumbing waste lines under every kitchen sink.

Kitchen sink plumbing repaired using duct tape.

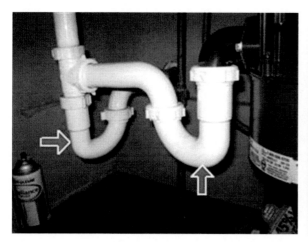

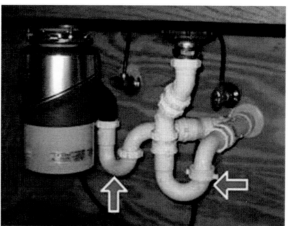

This drain has a double trap. This can cause air to be trapped between the two trap seals, and the "air-bound" drain will block the flow of water.

This drain also has a double trap.

PROBLEMS WITH GARBAGE DISPOSALS:

Properly installed electrical wires under the garbage disposal.

Check for rust on the top of the disposal where it connects to the sink. This is a common problem.

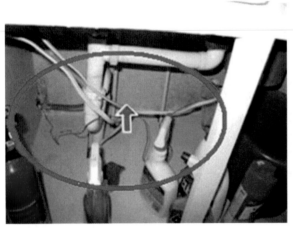

Romex wires to a garbage disposal should be run in armored, flexible cable for safety.

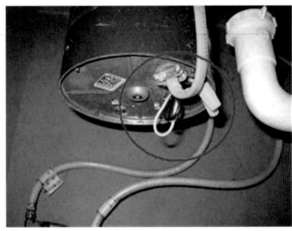

The garbage disposal should be properly wired, with the Romex wires hidden for safety.

PROBLEMS WITH GARBAGE DISPOSALS:

When installing a garbage disposal in an older home a new wire should be run directly from the main electrical panel. This one has its power coming from the outlet above and which is also powering the dishwasher and is an incorrect installation method. These wires should also be run in a protective armored cable.

This garbage disposal is not wired safely. The switch is missing a junction box cover and the electrical wire should be run in an armored cable for safety.

PROBLEMS WITH MICROWAVES:

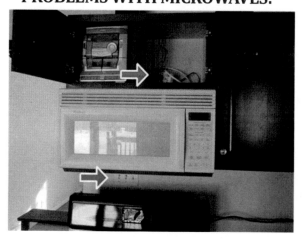 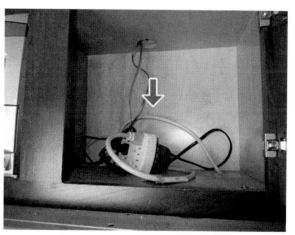

Always look above the microwave to see how the electrical outlet was installed. Technically, a microwave should be wired directly to the main panel on its own separate circuit breaker. This microwave was wired from the center light switch below the microwave and we discovered this when testing the lights. This is another example of a homeowner trying to do the work of a professional electrician.

Chapter 13
Interior-Room Inspection

When inspecting the interior of a home, you must look for several features. Look past the beauty of the home, and stay focused on the essentials of the inspection.

MUST-CHECK AREAS

1. INTERIOR FLOORS—Look closely at all floors in the home. Inspect the floors, especially near all exterior doors and sliding or French doors, as these are common places for wood rot. Using your body weight, step into the corners to determine if the floor is solid.

2. INTERIOR AND EXTERIOR DOORS—Check all interior and exterior doors to make sure they open and close properly and are free of damage. An interior door may stick when opening and closing, or the strike plates may need to be adjusted to hold the door closed.

3. WINDOWS—Open, close, lock, and unlock each window in the home. This check is very important, because windows often have either wood rot or other issues. It does not matter if the home is new or old. Look for water stains at the top of each interior window frame. Homeowners will repaint the trim on the sides and the bottom of a window but often forget to repaint the top where the water stains begin. Check all windows for broken thermal seals, which are apparent when the windows get foggy.

4. CEILINGS—Look very closely at all ceilings. First, look for water stains, which can occur in almost any room and in any spot. Look extra closely around every chimney, a common area for water leaks. Second, look for any drooping ceilings or drywall, a very common problem in homes that were built in the '70s and early '80s. Depending on the condition, the ceilings or drywall may need to be re-supported for safety.

5. WALLS—The interior walls will be in good condition most of the time. Minor cracks are normal inside homes. You should examine the wall under each window very closely, checking for past or current water leaks. Always check for water leaks in the wall that connects to the garage.

6. STAIRS AND RAILINGS—Check all stairs to make sure they are not loose, cracked, or damaged. Make sure that railings have been installed and that the stairs are secured to the wall.

7. SKYLIGHTS—Because skylights are common sources of water leaks, if the home has skylights look carefully at each of them, checking for water stains. The water stains may be due to excessive humidity from a humidifier being turned up too high. Also check a broken thermal seal in the glass, which would cause the glass to fog.

8. ATTIC FANS—If the home has an attic fan, open at least one window in the home before turning on the attic fan.

9. OUTLETS AND SWITCHES—Check all electrical outlets and light switches to make sure they are functional. Some of the electrical outlets may be set up to operate only when a light switch is turned on. In older homes it is common to find three-pronged electrical outlets that appear to be grounded but when actually tested prove to be ungrounded. We recommend that all ungrounded, three-pronged outlets be replaced with two-pronged ungrounded outlets. Another common electrical issue is the existence of outlets with reversed polarity. Reverse polarity is commonly found when homeowners have installed their own outlets. They have mistakenly reversed the negative black wire and the positive white wire and placed them on incorrect sides of the outlet.

10. TERMITES—We recommend that every home, whether inspected by a professional inspector or by you that it is inspected for termites by a termite company or a home inspection company.

PROBLEMS WITH INTERIOR CEILINGS AND WALLS:

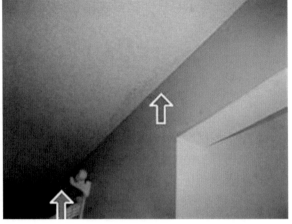

If you see a water stain on a drop ceiling, remove the ceiling tile and see if the leak is current.

Water stains on an interior ceiling frequently occur around the chimney. The chimney may be used only for the furnace or hot water heater, and may not be visible inside the home, but they run up through the walls and the attic to the exterior of the roof.

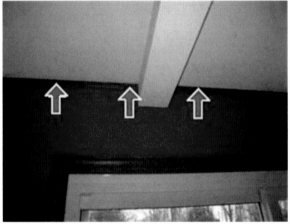

Check for ceiling and supporting walls that may be bowing. This photo shows an older home in which a wall was removed to make the room more open. The problem is, the installed support beam is undersized and its center has dropped approximately two inches.

This photo shows water stains on the interior wall ceiling. This can be caused by an exterior deck or vent, but if there is neither of these it is probably caused by ice jamming in the winter.

PROBLEMS WITH INTERIOR CEILINGS AND WALLS:

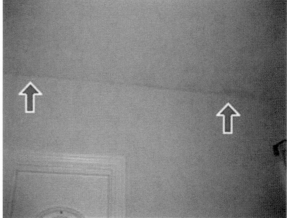

This picture shows water stains on a ceiling. Check all ceilings but especially those below bathrooms, kitchens, and any other running water.

This exterior was has a water stain. Such stains are generally caused by ice backup during the winter.

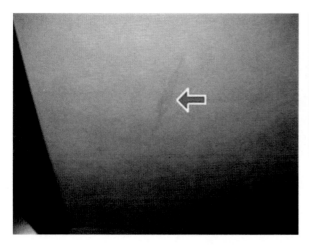

If a water stain is on a main-floor ceiling, what is directly above it? In a two-story home, the problem will generally come from the floor above.

This photo shows a water stain on a ceiling exterior wall.

PROBLEMS WITH INTERIOR CEILINGS AND WALLS:

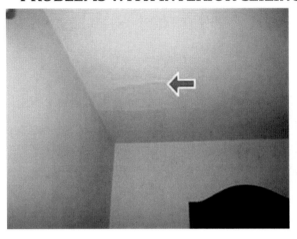
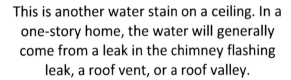

This is another water stain on a ceiling. In a one-story home, the water will generally come from a leak in the chimney flashing leak, a roof vent, or a roof valley.

This is a serious wall crack due to the size of the opening. When you see a crack like this you must start looking much more closely at the foundation in this area to determine what is making this happen.

This photo shows how pictures were hung many years ago. Many older homes have molding approximately one foot down from the ceiling for hanging picture frames in this way because pictures cannot otherwise be hung easily on plaster walls.

Always check for water stains directly under windows.

PROBLEMS WITH INTERIOR CEILINGS AND WALLS:

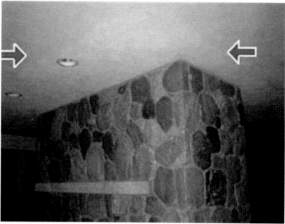

Water stains were found around this chimney. Such water stains are generally caused by a flashing leak around the chimney.

Check around the ceilings near fireplaces. The drywall in this picture has experienced water damage from a flashing leak on the roof and has been repaired. Look for wood rot in the chimney flashing and the sheathing in the attic around the chimney.

The ceiling drywall in this photo is sagging (difficult to see in the photo). Look closely at the ceilings, checking for any sagging drywall. Sagging drywall is a common problem in homes that were built in the late 1970s and early 1980s.

Here the drywall tape is bubbling up where the ceiling and the wall meet. Such bubbling is generally the result of a chimney flashing leak

PROBLEMS WITH INTERIOR FLOORS:

Check for wood rot in the floors near any sliding doors. You can do this by stepping next to the door frame and pressing along the entire interior of the door. If you find a soft area, revisit the basement area below, looking for any water stains on drywall, damaged wood, or rotted wood.

This floor shows signs of serious bowing. If you go look in the basement, you will find the problem. This home has two cracked floor joists and a main supporting beam that has twisted off to one side by approximately a half inch. These structural problems are cause for serious concern.

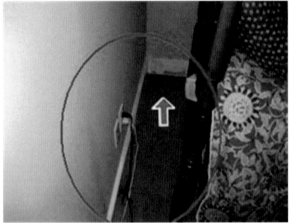

Always make sure you step on the floors next to the windows. In the laundry room of this new home, the floor directly below the window is rotted and will need to be replaced.

Here we see a water stain in the corner. You should look in corners behind all beds and furniture, especially the ones on exterior walls.

PROBLEMS WITH INTERIOR FLOORS:

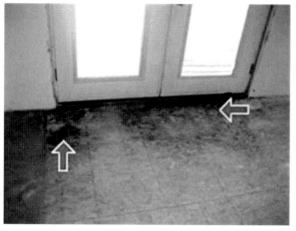 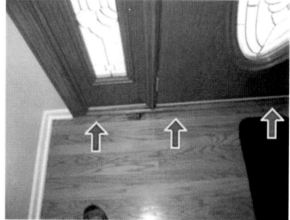

The floor around this front door has a serious water leak. If carpeting were installed, you would never notice this with just a superficial look. That is why it is so important to step next to all exterior doors to feel for wood rot and to look below every entry for water stains.	Water stains were found at the base of this entry door. There is a high probability the door is leaking water. Hire a licensed contractor to repair the door.

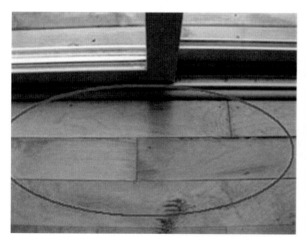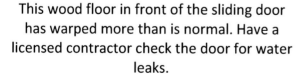 

This wood floor in front of the sliding door has warped more than is normal. Have a licensed contractor check the door for water leaks.	This is a photo of a new home in which we found water stains in the daylight basement area. Even if a home is new, it is important to look for leaks and water damage.

PROBLEMS WITH LIGHTS IN BASEMENTS AND CLOSETS:

Proper Type Of Lighting For Closets

Master bedroom closet light is a fire hazard and should be replaced with the proper light.

This is the proper type of florescent light fixture that should be installed in closets to prevent fire hazards.

When installing a light in a bedroom closet, use the proper florescent light fixture.

This extension cord runs to the main floor of the home where it is wired to a light fixture in a closet. Such improvised wiring is very dangerous.

Whenever you see a drop-down ceiling in a home, move the ceiling panel to the side and check whether the light fixture is wired properly and is using junction boxes to safely store the wires. Improper wiring is commonly found in basement lights.

PROBLEMS WITH INTERIOR WINDOWS:

Examine the window ledge under every window for water stains. Water will generally access from the top side of the windows and drip down on to the window ledge.

If you look closely at this window, you will see it is foggy, which would indicate that the window's thermal seal is broken. Thermal seals can cost as little as $100 per window to repair, or the window may need to be replaced.

This sliding door's thermal seal is broken.

This photo is from a newer home and one of the windows in the family room had bubbling paint, which indicates a water leak. Make sure you look at the top and bottom of every window.

PROBLEMS WITH INTERIOR WINDOWS:

This photo shows a window frame in which the bottom corner of the window has rotted. Open and close every window. If you see a water stain, push on it with your finger to determine whether it just a stain or wood rot.

Check the base of all basement windows for water stains.

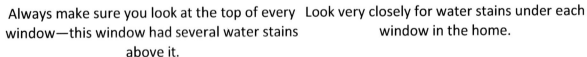

Always make sure you look at the top of every window—this window had several water stains above it.

Look very closely for water stains under each window in the home.

PROBLEMS WITH INTERIOR WINDOWS AND SKYLIGHTS:

Check every window to make sure locks are installed and operational for safety.

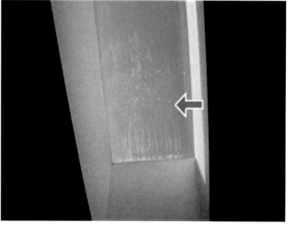

Common skylight problems are water leaks and broken thermal seals. A foggy skylight is often a sign of a broken thermal seal.

Open every window in the home, because you never know when you will open a window and find rot like this.

This window pane is cracked glass. Look closely at each window. Cracked glass can be easy to miss.

PROBLEMS WITH INTERIOR DOORS:

Check every interior door to make sure it opens and closes. Some doors in older homes may stick a little. This door would not close at all, and it was very tight at the top.

This door lock has been installed with the key lock on the interior, posing a safety hazard.

Look for wood rot at the base of each sliding door. Step on the floor near the doors to test for this.

Check that all doors are properly sealed.

PROBLEMS WITH INTERIOR RAILINGS, BANNISTERS, AND SPINDLES:

Any steps in a home need a mounted railing or a railing with spindles. The railing should be properly secured for safety.

Check for loose or broken railing spindles.

These stairs do not have a railing, and this poses a safety hazard.

Loose railings are common.

PROBLEMS WITH INTERIOR RAILINGS, BANNISTERS, AND SPINDLES:

Check the post of a railing system to see if it is loose. Posts that are not well secured are common problems.

This home is only two-years-old, but you should still inspect every spindle in its railing system. We found two spindles that had cracked and been glued back together.

Check all railings in the home. This railing is missing a spindle and the entire railing is loose, not an easy fix.

This staircase to the second floor is missing a railing.

Chapter 14
Bathroom Inspection

Bathroom items can be very expensive to repair or replace, so look closely for any bathroom problems.

MUST-CHECK AREAS:

1. BATHROOM FLOOR—When inspecting the bathroom floor, you need to check only a couple areas. The first is on both sides of the toilet, and the second is in both corners of the bathtub or shower unit. Step on these areas and use your body weight to check them for wood rot. Wood rot is not unusual in these areas, but it can be expensive to repair.

2. CEILING AND WALLS—When looking at the walls and ceilings, you may see a faint water streak. This is caused by not turning on the exhaust fan or not letting it run long enough to pull all the humidity out of the bathroom. The only way to repair the walls is to repaint them and afterward to habitually run the exhaust fan during the entire shower and for ten to fifteen minutes after you get out of the shower.

3. SINKS AND PLUMBING UNDER SINKS—Turn on all of the bathroom sinks. Let them run for a couple minutes and check for any water leaks around the faucets and below the sinks. Make sure there is plenty of water pressure. Make sure the sinks are draining properly. Many sinks drain very slowly and need to have the plumbing below them cleaned out.

4. SHUT-OFF VALVES—In today's construction, shut-off valves for water lines are installed under all bathroom sinks and toilets. Years ago this was not done, especially under sinks. Make sure that shut-off valves are installed in both these areas and that they are not leaking water. If the water to a toilet or sink has been turned off, it has generally been done because the shut-off valve has leaked in the past.

5. BATHROOM OUTLETS—Based on today's safety standards, we recommend that all bathroom outlets be GFCI outlets. These are the outlets with reset buttons.

6. BATHROOM FANS—Based on today's standards, we recommend that all bathrooms have exhaust fans vented to the exterior of the home. It is very common to find bathroom fans that were installed by the homeowner and never vented to the exterior. Take the time to go outside the home to find the exhaust fan vent, which should be located on the side of the home or in the soffit area near the bathroom. They are sometimes found exhausting into the attic rather than to the exterior, but this practice is incorrect.

7. BATHROOM SHOWERS—Turn on the water in each shower for approximately five minutes to make sure there is plenty of water pressure, the shower drains properly, and the showerhead does not leak. Make sure the tub stopper is functional. We recommend that you not walk away and start inspecting other areas while the bathtub is running, because if the bathtub does not drain properly it can fill with water very quickly and make a serious mess.

8. SHOWER SURROUNDS—If the home has a tiled shower, look very closely at the shower surround, checking for cracks, missing grout, and areas that have been repaired. These could be areas of great concern, requiring basic or even major repairs. Run the water for five minutes and check for water leaks in the room below the shower. Make sure the shower door opens and closes properly and that it does not leak water. It is common to see the base of the door heavily caulked because of past water leaks. Finally, look at the light fixture to make sure it is the proper type of fixture for showers.

BATHROOM GFCI OUTLETS

Bathroom GFCI Outlet
Properly Installed

Test all bathroom outlets to make sure they are GFCI-protected for safety. Remember, not all the bathroom outlets will have reset buttons on them to indicate that they are GFCI-protected. Sometimes an outlet may be connected to a GFCI outlet in another bathrooms or to a GFCI electrical breaker in the main electrical panel. Bathrooms in older homes often have non-GFCI outlets consistent with the standard at that time.

PROBLEMS WITH BATHROOM SINKS AND DRAINS:

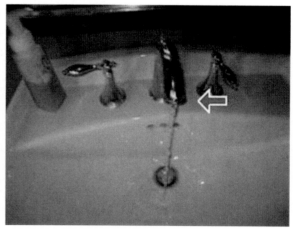

A bathroom sink draining very slowly usually means that the trap below is blocked and will need to be cleaned.

This bathroom sink had very low water pressure. In this situation the first thing you should check is that the screen under the faucet is clean. The majority of the time that is the only problem.

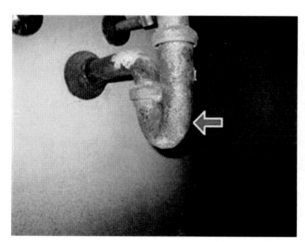

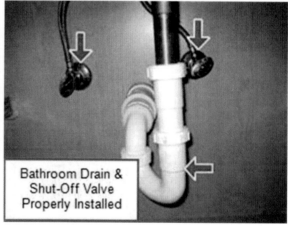

This is a photo of a metal drain trap under a bathroom sink. Feel around the bottom of these, because they are often rusted out and very close to having a serious leak. Be careful, though, because you may put a hole in the line because it was already so close to rusting completely through.

This photo shows shut-off valves that were installed under the bathroom sink. We recommend having shut-off valves under all faucets.

PROBLEMS WITH BATHROOM SINKS, DRAINS, AND SHUT-OFF VALVES:

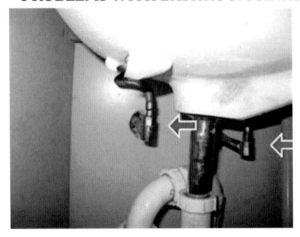

This bathroom sink is missing a shut-off valve. A shut-off valve is not a requirement, but it is helpful if the sink has a leak or the faucet needs to be replaced. Based on today's standards, we recommend that each water line have a shut-off valve.

The drain flange under a bathroom sink is a common area for water leaks to occur. The drain flange is for the built-in sink plug or stopper located above in the sink.

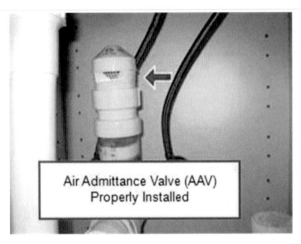

Air Admittance Valve (AAV)
Properly Installed

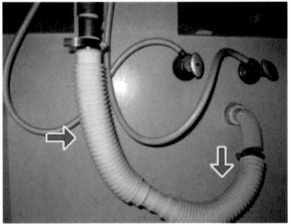

Air admittance valves (AAV) are pressure-activated, one-way, mechanical valves used in a plumbing system to eliminate the need for conventional pipe venting through the roof system. They are frequently found in older homes but are only used under bathroom sinks or kitchen sinks.

This is not the correct way to run bathroom plumbing.

PROBLEMS WITH FLOORS NEAR BATHTUBS AND TOILETS:

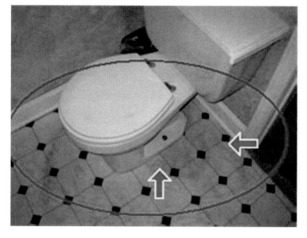

Check that the bathroom floor where it meets the toilet has been properly caulked. For tile, use tile caulk available from your local hardware store.

There are water stains around this toilet. Check the floor around the toilet for wood rot. Check both sides of each toilet by stepping on the floor around the toilet.

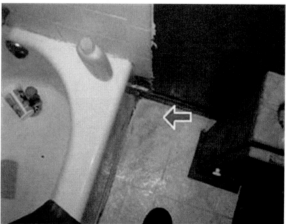

This should be caulked where the floor and tub meet.

Wood rot found in the corner of the bathroom where the tub and floor come together.

PROBLEMS WITH BATHTUBS AND SHOWER SURROUNDS:

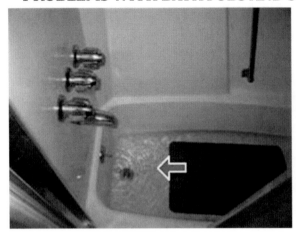

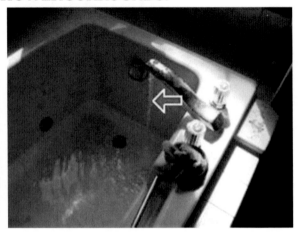

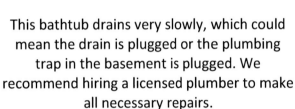

This bathtub drains very slowly, which could mean the drain is plugged or the plumbing trap in the basement is plugged. We recommend hiring a licensed plumber to make all necessary repairs.

This bathtub has very low water pressure, which could mean the faucet is not functioning properly or the water line feeding the tub is plugged (galvanized pipes are the only type of water line typically subject to becoming plugged). We recommend hiring a licensed plumber to make all necessary repairs.

This shower is brand-new and was installed by a homeowner (a flipper). The problem is that the three shower heads are located directly in the center of the shower doors and they leak through the door and onto the bathroom floor when being turned on. You should run each shower to look for water leaks.

This brand-new home's shower surround is leaking water. When testing for leaks, you should try to run water up against the shower's glass wall. Sometimes even though you run water like this you won't find any leaks until you actually take a shower.

PROBLEMS WITH BATHTUBS AND SHOWER SURROUNDS:

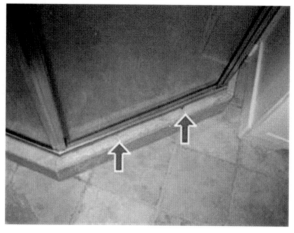

An older shower pan needs to be caulked around its base as part of regular maintenance. Run the water for five to ten minutes and check for leaks in the ceiling below the shower. Don't walk away from the shower until you know it does not leak.

This is another photo of a new shower door leaking water. Run every shower and check closely for leaks.

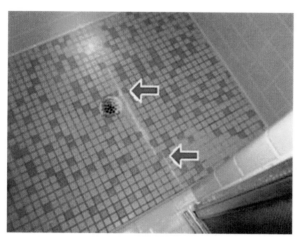

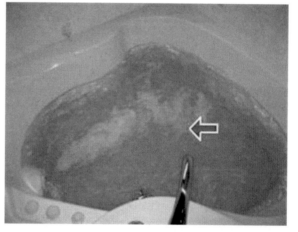

There is a large crack in the center of this shower pan. In this situation, we recommend running the water and looking for any water leaks directly below the shower. Oftentimes these are just cracks in the tile floor, but it is very important to check if the cracks have caused leaks.

If you fill a bathroom tub and the water is discolored like in this photo, turn the water off, drain the tub, and refill it. Sometimes if the water has not been run for a while at that location it will come out discolored. If the water is still discolored when you fill the bathtub for the second time, you most likely need a water softener. Call a professional to test the water.

PROBLEMS WITH BATHTUBS AND SHOWER SURROUNDS:

Jacuzzi Bathtub

This shower diverter does not operate properly. When you pull up on the shower diverter, the shower should turn on. Repairing a shower diverter is generally inexpensive, but shower diverters should be checked in every home inspection.

If the home has a Jacuzzi or whirlpool bathtub, you should fill the bathtub and run the jets to make sure it is operates properly. These types of bathtubs should be plugged into a GFCI outlet under the bathtub or run directly to a GFCI electrical breaker in the main electrical panel.

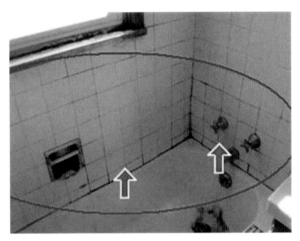

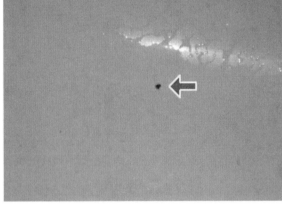

This shower's surrounding walls have rotted. The only way to test for rot is to push on the tiles. If you can feel the tiles push in, you know there is wood rot behind them.

This bathtub has a small chip or crack. Chips and cracks are common and can be repaired.

PROBLEMS WITH SHOWERS AND DRAINS:

This beautiful, new shower was installed next to an exterior wall of a bathroom in a remodeled home. In many climates this location would not be an issue, but in colder climates the water lines may freeze so this location would not be recommended.

This home is a high-end foreclosure that has been remodeled by professionals, but the shower still would not drain. It is very important to check bathtubs and showers in every home no matter how new or newly remodeled.

PROBLEMS WITH BATHROOM EXHAUST FANS AND LIGHTING:

1. We recommend all bathrooms have bathroom fans that are vented directly to the exterior of the home. A bathroom in an older home may not have a fan, but it should at least have an operational window.
2. We recommend checking all bathroom lights and bathroom heat lights to make sure that they are functional.

The owners of this home ran the basement bathroom exhaust through the furnace's fresh-air intake line. This was done by the homeowner because it is much easier than running the bathroom exhaust directly to the exterior as should have been done. Fresh-air intake lines are needed in homes today, which are built airtight: these lines bring fresh air back into the home as needed for the heating systems to operate properly.

PROBLEMS WITH BATHROOM EXHAUST FANS, CEILINGS AND LIGHTING:

This much chipping paint without water stains generally means that the ceiling was painted without first applying primer.

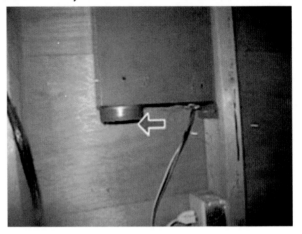

Look above the bathroom ceiling, if accessible, to see whether the exhaust fan has been run to the exterior of the home. If you cannot see above the ceiling, walk to the exterior of the home near the shower and look for an exhaust fan vent outside.

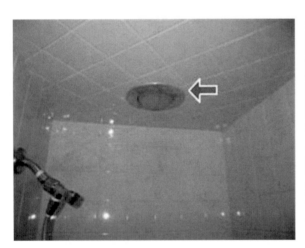

The light fixture in this shower is not water-safe, so it poses a safety hazard.

Older homes will sometimes still have pull chain light fixtures in kitchens, bathrooms, and laundry. This is a safety hazard near water.

Chapter 15
Laundry-Room Inspection

The laundry room is typically small, but you still need to check it thoroughly for any problems.

MUST-CHECK AREAS:

1. GAS OR ELECTRIC—Determine whether the home has gas dryer, an electric dryer, or the option for both.

2. DRYER VENT—Look behind the dryer to check if the dryer vent is installed properly. We recommend that a dryer vent be run in a metal line rather than a soft plastic line. Many homeowners use plastic line because it is easy to install, and they use way too much of it, causing poor air flow which prevents the dryer from venting and operating efficiently.

3. ELECTRICAL—If the home is older, inspect the electrical outlet near the washer and dryer to make sure it is a three-prong grounded outlet. The best way to test it is to use an electrical outlet tester.

4. LAUNDRY TUB AND FAUCETS—If the home has a laundry tub, check for leaks around the faucet and under the laundry tub's drain. For safety make sure the outlet near the laundry tub is GFCI-protected.

PROBLEMS WITH GAS AND ELECTRIC DRYER EXHAUST:

1. Check that the dryer is vented to the exterior of the home. We recommend that all dryer exhausts be run in metal lines. Although flexible lines are acceptable, they tend to have dips that cause dryer-lint to back up. We also recommend that the dryer lines be cleaned by a duct-cleaning company every couple years.

2. Check whether the dryer is gas, electric, or has the option for both.

PROBLEMS WITH GAS AND ELECTRIC DRYER EXHAUST:

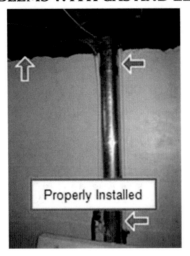

This dryer vent has been properly installed using a metal dryer vent.

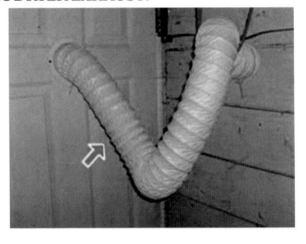

We prefer that all laundry exhausts be run in metal vent lines rather than plastic vent lines, so would recommend that this vent line be replaced.

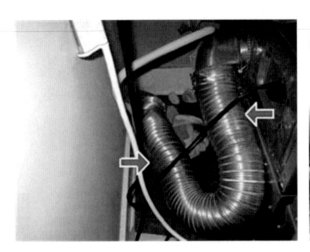

This dryer vent line should be shortened and run directly to the exterior of the home. We do not recommend having many elbows or turns in the line.

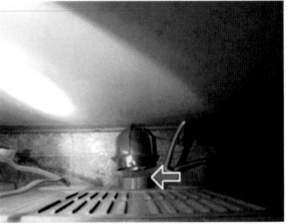

This dryer vent line is disconnected. You should always look behind the dryer to check that the exhaust is hooked up properly.

PROBLEMS WITH GAS AND ELECTRIC DRYER EXHAUST:

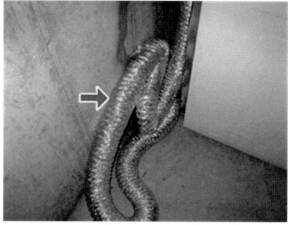

Check the dryer exhaust cover on the exterior of the home to make sure it has a louvered cover, as this one does. Unfortunately, this one is it is very dirty and should be cleaned.

This is probably the worst installation of a dryer vent line we have ever seen.

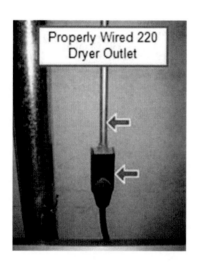

This is a photo of a properly wired 220 dryer plug with a dryer plugged into it.

This old gas line is kinked or bent. We recommend replacing this old type of gas dryer line with a new, flexible line.

PROBLEMS WITH GAS DRYER LINES AND ELECTRICAL PLUGS:

This photo shows a gas line to a dryer. The gas line should be secured to the wall for safety.

Make sure that all electrical outlets for laundry appliances are grounded. This one is a three-prong outlet, but it is not grounded. Ungrounded laundry outlets are often found in older homes. This outlet is also missing its face plate, which poses an additional safety hazard.

 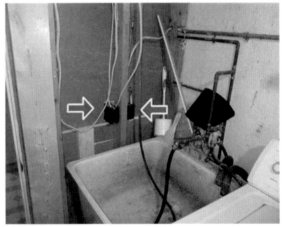

This one is very difficult to see but this is a non-grounded two prong outlet directly above a clothes washer. This outlet should be rewired with a three prong grounded outlet for safety.

A proper water resistant wall should be installed to protect these electrical boxes from moisture from the sink. This is a safety hazard.

Chapter 16
Fireplace Inspection

We recommend that a natural, wood-burning fireplace or a wood-burning fireplace that has been converted to gas-burning be inspected by a professional chimney sweep. The fireplace must be cleaned and in complete working order before you use it, because it can be very expensive to repair.

MUST-CHECK AREAS:

1. FIREPLACE LINER—To the best of your ability, look at the fireplace chimney liner of a wood-burning fireplace to see whether it has been cleaned and to check it for cracks. Determining if the chimney liner is cracked is very difficult when it is covered in creosol. We recommend hiring a professional chimney sweep to clean the chimney and inspect the liner and chimney.

2. FIREPLACE DAMPER—The fireplace damper is the door you would open to look all the way up the chimney. Make sure that the damper is operational; if not operational, it should be repaired.

3. FIRE BRICKS—The interior walls of a fireplace are made of fire bricks. Check the fire bricks to see if they have moved or cracked. Again, we recommend fireplaces be inspected by a professional chimney sweep.

4. GAS-BURNING FIREPLACE—Gas-burning fireplaces can be difficult to light if the home has been vacant for a long time or if the fireplace has not been used by the residents. We recommend you try to light each gas-burning fireplace to make sure it functions properly. If a gas-burning fireplace already has a lit pilot, check that a damper clip is installed. A damper clip is a small U-shaped piece of metal attached to the damper that keeps the damper open approximately a half inch to allow the pilot gas to dissipate upward through the chimney. Before turning on the fireplace, make sure the damper is wide open. When you're finished testing the fireplace, close the damper.

5. FIREPLACE HEARTH—Check that the fireplace hearth is sound, with no loose bricks, and that the mantel is secure.

PROBLEMS WITH WOOD-BURNING FIREPLACES AND WOOD-BURNING STOVES:

The tile on this fireplace hearth is loose. This is a common problem. Look closely at all of the hearth tiles to check if they are cracked or loose.

This chimney damper is broken. You should crouch down and look up at the chimney fireplace damper to make sure it operates properly and is not damaged.

This dirty firebox should be cleaned.

Every chimney should be cleaned and inspected by a professional chimney sweep before a new owner moves into the home.

PROBLEMS WITH WOOD-BURNING FIREPLACES AND WOOD-BURNING STOVES:

Even if a fireplace looks really clean, like this one does, crouch down, open the damper, and make sure you can see all the way up the flue.

This fireplace mantel is loose.

It is difficult to see in this photo, but the fire bricks have pushed in toward the fireplace. When you see something like this, call a professional chimney sweep to make all necessary repairs.

Wood-burning stoves are great, but you should have them cleaned and inspected by a professional chimney sweep before moving into a home. Most home inspectors will not check wood-burning stoves.

PROBLEMS WITH WOOD-BURNING FIREPLACES:

The fireplace in this home was starting to lean toward the outside of the home. This is the is the front view of fireplace where it meets the ceiling. In the next photo to the right you will see a side view.

The fireplace in this home was starting to lean toward the outside of the home. We noticed this by looking at the top of the fireplace where it meets the ceiling.

For safety, a fireplace mantel must be secured to the fireplace.

The owner of this home added a room with a wall less than one foot from a fireplace. The proximity poses a safety hazard.

PROBLEMS WITH GAS FIREPLACES AND EXHAUST:

Gas Fireplace

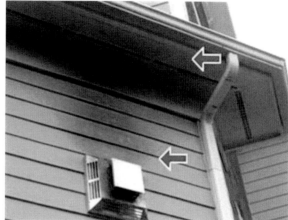

We recommend that you test each gas-burning fireplace to make sure it operates properly. If it has not been used in a long time, it may take a little time to start. Some of these fireplaces can be dangerous to light, so be cautious, and if you don't feel completely safe starting it for the first time, call a professional chimney sweep.

The gas fireplace in this home is burning exhaust and burning much too rich, causing the black discoloration above the exhaust vent. We recommend hiring a company that specializes in gas-burning fireplaces.

Chapter 17
Termite Inspection

1. Having a termite inspection performed by a home inspector or a termite extermination company is a very important part of purchasing a home. It is amazing how many different homes we find termites in every year. All homes should be inspected for termites. It does not matter if the home has been sided with vinyl, concrete, wood, brick or any other product. Home interiors typically still have wood framing in the walls and floors which termites have a way of finding and destroying.

2. Walk the entire home exterior and look closely where the siding and the ground come together. You want to make sure that the ground and the siding have a minimum of 6 inches between the two of them, or it will be an open invite for termites to invade your home.

3. Make sure whenever you see a pile of wood stacked next to the home that you look closely around the wood pile and in the basement or crawlspace near the wood pile.

4. Look for round drill holes on the foundation, walkway or patio where the home has been treated in the past for termites.

5. Some of the most common ways we find termites is coming from the font, back and side porches and patios, so look very closely around and under these areas in your basement and crawlspace.

6. When inspecting the basement and crawlspaces look very closely at every floor joist, sill plate, rim joist, supporting beam and in-between every supporting beam. Finding termites in a basement or crawlspace is truly a matter of being thorough in your inspection.

7. Walk around the interior of the home and inspect all the baseboard trim and the wall. Just because you did not find termites in the basement does not mean you will not find them on the main floor, second floor or even in the attic.

SIGNS OF TERMITES:

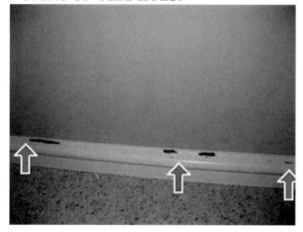

These are signs of termites in this two-year-old home, so if you think a new home doesn't need a termite inspection you could be seriously wrong. Seeing a termite problem when you are inside the home may be difficult. For example, when we first saw this it was an off-colored white, but running a finger across it caused the termite problems to appear.

This is a photo of a wooden main support beam in a basement. Check wooden support beams for rot or termite infestation by looking from below and up into the floor joist then pushing up against it with a large screwdriver.

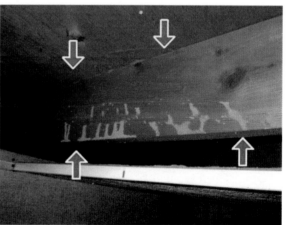

The white lines in this photo, indicated by the arrows, are signs of termites.

This photo is of termite infestation on a floor joist in a basement.

SIGNS OF TERMITES:

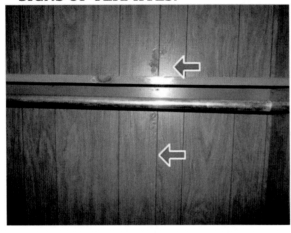

This paneled wall appears to have some bubbling in it, but the bubbling is actually termite infestation. Look closely and touch anything on a wall that appears odd.

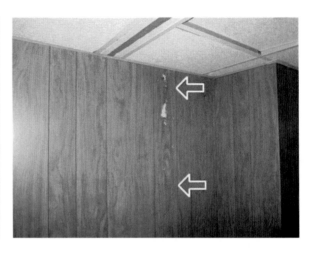

The arrows in this photo are pointing to termite infestation in the paneling.

We found termites in the basement of this home. Then we went to the laundry room directly above and found its floor was rotted from the termites and needed to be replaced.

The white lines in this photo, indicated by the arrows, are signs of termites.

SIGNS OF TERMITES:

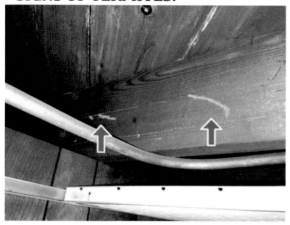

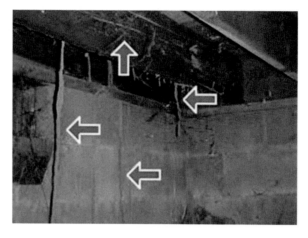

When you think that the home you're buying is a brick home and you don't need a termite inspection, think again. This home's exterior siding was 100% brick and was loaded with termites.

The white spots and lines on the wooden joists are signs of termites.

TERMITE TREATMENTS:

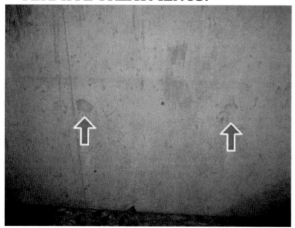

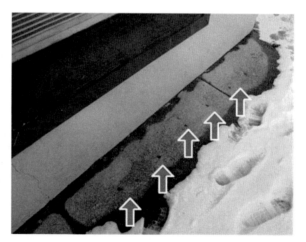

Round holes like these in a basement or crawl space and wrapping around the foundation are generally signs that the home has been treated for termites.

This photo shows the holes that were drilled on the exterior of the home to treat for termites, these holes should have been sealed up with concrete, we recommend when you see something like this you have a professional termite company re inspect the home.

The Home Inspection Guide for Do-It-Yourself Home Buyers

Chapter 18
Conclusion

Thank you for purchasing "The Home Inspection Guide for Do-It-Yourself Home Buyers." We hope it has been an effective, informative and helpful book in your home buying experience. We have endeavored to provide you with as much helpful information as possible, while keeping the book at a reasonable page count and the information in a form that easy to understand and implement.

There is an important reminder we would like to leave you with. We would like to stress that there is a very important rule to live by as you proceed through the home buying process, and you have seen it repeated so many times throughout the text of this book: when in doubt, call or hire a professional. Two hundred pages of photos or two thousand pages of technical writing will not make you a professional, nor will it cover every possible issue, concern or warning sign possible during a home inspection. Only with years of real world experience will you be able to properly inspect a home and fully understand if the purchase you are about to make is a good one.

We wish you the very best as you move forward with your home purchase. If you have questions or feedback, we would love to hear from you. Please connect with us at our official website: **www.DoItYourselfHomeInspections.com.**

Page
210